CW01560353

Class at Work

Work and Society in the Eighties

Series Editor: Michael Rose
*Senior Lecturer, School of Humanities and Social Sciences
and Associate Fellow, Centre for European Industrial
Studies, University of Bath*

This series aims to present authoritative treatments of
key aspects of work, in its role as a central social and
historical phenomenon in human life. All volumes are
written by specialists in the appropriate fields, but in
such a way that together they will provide interlocking
coverage of concepts, controversies, and major trends in
a variety of academic subject areas concerned with work
issues. At the same time, they supply valuable
documentation on the movement of values, action and
structures in advanced societies in general. Students will
find the series especially helpful, but it will also challenge
professionals in management and industrial relations to
review their own practice, provide teachers and
researchers with stimulating new interpretations, and
come to the aid of general readers wishing to be fully
informed about the subject.

Already published:

Authority and Participation in Industry
Peter Brannen

CLASS
AT
WORK

The Design, Allocation & Control of Jobs

CRAIG R. LITTLER
& GRAEME SALAMAN

BATSFORD ACADEMIC AND EDUCATIONAL LTD
London

For Gill and Rena

Typeset by Progress Filmsetting Ltd
Printed and bound in Great Britain
by Billing & Sons Limited Worcester
for the publishers
Batsford Academic and Educational Ltd
4 Fitzhardinge Street, London W1H 0AH

British Library Cataloguing in Publication Data

Littler, Craig
    Class at work.
    1. Work — Social aspects
    I. Title II. Salaman, Graeme
    306'.36 HD6955

ISBN 0 7134 4385 5

ISBN 0 7134 4386 3 Pbk

Contents

Editor's Foreword

Authors in this series have been encouraged to enliven their exposition with empirical data drawn from current social research and debate. Such a practice in turn demands compression and selectivity in conceptual and theoretical discussion. In the text that follows the authors have stated their views on political economy, and its relation to workplace life, in a concise and challenging form. Readers will find much to provoke and stimulate them in what many should find an enjoyable blending of theory and factual evidence.

The treatment turns upon the existence of systematic inequalities in the workplace. To the authors these are most readily comprehensible as the result of economic exploitation occurring under capitalist economic institutions as the latter function *at present*. The stress is necessary because 'exploitation', in its technical rather than its emotive sense, has occurred in some form or another under all known existing economic systems of any complexity, and in particular under all forms of industrialism. The simplest explanation of why this is so is that all industrialised countries employ, in whatever complex or modified forms, a variety of payment systems in which a wage or salary is paid in reward for a level of effort that in most cases is never exactly specified, agreed, or understood. In cases of disagreement, superior power will finally decide the issue, and in general it is the employer who holds such power. Exploitation, however, should not automatically be equated with 'extortion', or 'degradation'; it is, rather, a process whereby an employer purchases the right to utilise an employee's capacity to work, and will then tend to seek a maximum output, but will not always do so consistently, or with great effectiveness.

Despite this qualification, no inconsistency arises in claiming that workers earning three or four times the national average wage, without undue exertion, may nevertheless be viewed as exploited workers. By the same token, exploitation will remain a feature of state socialist countries no less than of market-oriented societies so long as the former retain wage-payment systems in some form. But features of capitalist industrialism — its orientation towards private profit and accumulation, its legal stress on individualism, its historical evolution, etc. — set it apart from alternative social models which may be viewed either as attractive or appalling.

Workplace inequalities can be viewed, under capitalism, as a structured source, and an expression, of broader disparities — some no more than half-consciously perceived by subjects — that nourish class antagonism. The authors do not shirk the task of tracing the bases of this underlying class conflict. Yet, as they point out in an important passage worth quoting in full:

> Remaining at the level of abstract assertion of formal class antagonisms results . . . in a vitiated analysis of work relations for a number of reasons . . . it eliminates any need to investigate actual worker-management relations . . . it fails to attach importance to worker attitudes and motivations by regarding them as irrelevant. It thus leads to a conception of control which accords no significance to management efforts — by various devices — to generate some level of consent. (p.58).

Blatantly accentuated inequalities might render workforces openly rebellious, or at best leave them so disaffected and dismotivated that the cost and inconvenience of controlling them, by increasingly autocratic techniques, soon rise to an intolerable level. Yet there exists a strong current of opinion, based upon powerful gut-feelings amongst advantaged groups, that a general increase of inequalities, at work as elsewhere, would have a tonic effect on productivity. Persons holding such views will find this text unsympathetic to their beliefs, if only because it argues very strongly indeed that inequalities in the workplace seem to remain greater and more persistent than has been widely asserted. Whether an accentuation of inequalities in workplaces would redynamise the economy, or would, rather, redynamise the labour movement, or would, just possibly, do both, is a question which the authors wisely leave to the political professionals.

Michael Rose
University of Bath

Acknowledgements

It is the least we can do, in a book about work organisation, to acknowledge the assistance and support which has helped to make this book possible. Much of our early collaborative work (which culminated in a joint article in *Sociology* in 1982) was financed by grants from the Social Science Faculty at the Open University and we would like to express our gratitude to the research committee of the faculty. This book is the product of that earlier collaboration but in this book we move beyond the preoccupations of that article.

We would also like to thank the following publishers for permission to reproduce material: Pluto Press for Table 1 on p.30; Routledge and Kegan Paul for Figure 1, p.108; New Left Review for Table 1, p.109; and Cambridge University Press for Table 2, p.111.

In academic terms we are grateful for the support and interest of our colleagues at Imperial College and the Open University, particularly those members of the sociology seminar at the Open University. During the course of the writing of the book, Tony Seward of Batsford, and Michael Rose made useful comments on earlier drafts. Jac Sykes helped us enormously by collecting recent statistics for Chapter 2, and Marie Day worked diligently and patiently on many drafts, transforming our messy manuscripts into coherent typescripts — many thanks.

Craig Littler
Graeme Salaman

1 · Introduction

We have given this book the title 'Class at Work' because it both conjures up a number of ideas, processes and relationships and allows us to treat them together. The conception of class at work examined first is probably the most popular one. This is the level and form of analysis presented in the first chapter — what we have called the distributive, tangible aspects of class at work. Chapter 2 describes, in empirical and up-to-date detail, the nature and extent of class differences and inequalities as these are experienced at work. The chapter outlines class differences in 'life chances' as they arise through different locations within employing organisations. In many ways this is the most important sense in which the expression 'class at work' can be used, for it describes real, concrete circumstances and experiences, which impinge, one way or another, on us all. But in another sense this level of definition is only the surface of a deeper reality. Chapter 3 attempts to expose this more structural, hidden aspect of class at work. It seeks to show how the phenomena described in Chapter 2 are the result of the working out of other forces, of competitive pressure, market pressure, urging each firm constantly and unremittingly to be profitable, to be more profitable, never to relax from the threat, real or anticipated, of competitive disadvantage. The pressures on firms to be and to remain profitable (especially in a time of recession) force them, as Chapter 3 argues, constantly to seek new ways of increasing their share of the product relative to labour. In other words, for firms to seek, as they are required to do, to be more profitable (regardless of how blandly this requirement might be expressed in the language of rationalisation, modernisation, new technologies) inevitably occasions an attempt to re-order class relations to capital's advantage.

This is the second, deeper sense in which the book analyses class at work, through a consideration of the working out of class pressures and forces in and on the enterprise. We pay particular attention to the implications of external market pressures for management's concern to reorganise internal organisational processes — especially the processes of work design and control. And it is these two internal processes which we regard as the third aspect of class at work.

The forces and interests of classes can be seen at work within the enterprise in relations between class categories. The enterprise constitutes a major arena within which class relations occur. Consider this analysis:

'The existence of widespread discontent among a large proportion of our working population, and the constant friction which results from it, are among the most serious obstacles to efficiency in production, and therefore to trade revival... It is useless to deny the legitimacy of the grievances from which unrest springs, or to assume that they are the consequences of economic forces beyond our control; men... will not permanently accept what they believe to be unjust because they are told it is inevitable.' (Liberal Industrial Inquiry, 1928). That diagnosis was made in the twenties, but its conclusions are familiar to us today: the existence of discontent at work is a consequence of work arrangements, relationships and experiences, and is a major factor influencing relations between workers and employers, and the manner in which management organises work and structures work and control.

This third sense of class at work, by focusing on relations between *classes* at work, reveals a number of contradictions and ironies. One we have already noted: the existence of 'discontent' both follows from work arrangements and is a causal factor in influencing management's choice of work arrangements. This level of paradox has been analysed perceptively by Alan Fox in his book *Beyond Contract*. In this book, Fox (1974) explores the spiral of distrust between workers and managers, whereby managers' conception of workers as untrustworthy, once institutionalised in tightly prescribed rules and work specifications, creates the effects on which it is based and thus leads to a further withdrawal of goodwill and necessitates a further increase in regulation – a continuing vicious circle.

There is however a further level of contradiction which has not been so fully documented and which constitutes the major focus of the last three chapters of the book. The contradiction is identified in Chapter 4. Essentially it is this: the enterprise, quite obviously, reveals at one and the same time relations of co-operation and integration, and relations of conflict and exploitation. This dual aspect of work relations has been emphasised recently by Cressey and MacInnes (1980), Burawoy (1979) and Littler and Salaman (1982). However, this aspect of work relations has not been fully explored, in spite of its significance and centrality, and in particular has not been analysed in terms of its implications for control procedures and mechanisms, and for work design and work technology. This is the function of the last three chapters of the book.

That relations between workers and management are at the same time both co-operative and full of conflict is probably obvious to anyone who has ever worked in a factory or office, and is obvious to anyone who has followed the recent literature on work and work organisation. But its implications have not always been fully grasped. The bases for conflict at work are clear, from Chapter 2, which documents work-based inequalities, and from Chapter 3 which identifies the structural conflict of interests which exists between workers and management within the capitalist enterprise, regardless of the philosophies or personal predispositions of either party. At the same time, the sheer weight and pervasiveness of co-operation is equally, if not more obvious. Most employees, most of the time, are not in a state of resistance to or conflict with their employers. Indeed most places of work most of the time are striking for the degree to which people get on with their work without constant surveillance, supervision, or coercion. Yet *both* these forms of relationship are real, and both are, in one form or another, constantly present.

They are both particularly real to the employer. As Chapter 4 argues, following recent analyses, the employer is caught in an unresolveable dilemma: although in essence his relations with his staff are (a) highly inequalitarian (see Chapter 2) and (b) ultimately relations of conflict, in that the interests of each party pull in different directions, yet he relies on the continuing goodwill and co-operation of his employees. The first aspect of the relationship between employer and employee – that they are inequalitarian relations of conflict and exploitation – leads the employer to develop forms of work and control which maximise the productivity of labour, make it as unskilled as is feasible, cheapen it and regulate it so that workers are constrained to act according to the specifications of the employer. *But* at the same time such tendencies create an increasingly serious disadvantage: the loss of employee goodwill, the emergence of worker resistance, and high levels of labour turnover and absenteeism. This development not only results in a further twist to the spiral of mistrust and regulation described by Fox: it also has practical consequences for worker productivity, morale, and flexibility. In other words, the basic nature of the worker/employer relationship within capitalism tends to result in the emergence of work forms which themselves threaten the profitability and productivity of the enterprise in the long term.

Chapters 5 and 6 consider this contradiction in the light of recent developments in work design and work technology. These chapters seek to encapsulate the essence of past job design, to describe current trends and to locate these in terms of an apparent oscillation between poles of trust and autonomy, mistrust and repression, within the imperatives which impinge on any capitalist enterprise – to be profitable, competitive, and to gain and control a share of the market. In this vein, Chapter 6 examines the present realities of the age old employer dream of the unmanned factory and the elimination of labour, as a *transformation* of the problem of control and compliance.

It is in these two chapters that we seek to demonstrate the value and validity of the approach and subject matter of the book. For the title is intended to suggest that class is not simply a way of describing work arrangements and circumstances, however important and disgraceful these may be, but that class is also a way of understanding work arrangements and tendencies – that class is real, not simply in that it has very real consequences, as Chapter 1 demonstrates, but in that it is a constant dynamic, the origin of the processes and contradictions which 'work out' in a number of ways at work, and which this book attempts to analyse.

2 · The Inequalities of Working Life

Work is of two kinds: first altering the position of matter at or near the earth's surface relatively to other such matter; second telling other people to do so. The first kind is unpleasant and ill-paid; the second is pleasant and highly-paid.

The second kind is capable of indefinite extension: there are not only those who give orders, but those who give advice as to what orders should be given.

Bertrand Russell, *In Praise of Idleness*, 1932

This book is concerned to delineate the major dynamics and features of work organisation. As will be seen in subsequent chapters, this concern leads us to focus on the contradiction within work organisation and experience between the need for control and the need for consent, between the need to regulate and dominate production, but also that of engaging the enthusiasm and willingness of those who sell their labour. This conflict is 'resolved' in different ways at different times, but such resolutions are subject to constant destabilisation by pressures from competitors, technological developments, changes in worker militancy, or other factors (including political developments). We analyse this contradiction and attempt to locate it within the dynamics of capitalist economies, and to understand current tendencies which have an impact on organisations' efforts, and ability, to resolve such problems. Later chapters explore the contradiction in terms of work design principles and developments, and the utilisation of new technologies.

But first we must consider another basic feature of work experience and organisation which has a key significance in the development of the contradiction which constitutes the major theme of our analysis. The world of work and organisation can of course be seen in various ways: as the area of production, where goods and services are produced; as the source of wealth — personal incomes and spending power; as an area of effort, experiment, initiative as businesses rise, prosper, decline. But the most glaring feature of work, the feature which must strike any casual visitor as dramatically as it strikes the diligent researcher, is that work is a world of inequality. Work rewards, deprivations, dangers, frustrations, satisfactions are distributed highly unequally.

Now this has an obvious implication for our theme. We are interested in the dynamics of control, and the contradiction between employers needing to control and organise their employees and the fact that their efforts to do so are likely to make them even less controllable. Such a possibility is likely to be greatly enhanced if, as is the case, the employees suffer not only the restraints of regulation and loss of autonomy, but are also disadvantaged, relative to their controllers or employers, in a whole variety of other dimensions — such as financial rewards and working conditions.

For this reason alone — that inequalities of numerous sorts coincide with differences in organisational power, with the distinction between controllers and controlled — we are concerned to delineate the nature and extent of these work-based inequalities. But there is much more. These inequalities, we shall argue, are not haphazard or random. They are themselves the consequences of differences in interest between managers and managed. They are not, in other words, simply additional to this distinction, they are *part of the distinction* itself. The considerable inequalities that exist between controllers and controlled reflect the conflict of interest between these two camps and the differential power of each camp — and its external allies — to achieve its interest in the face of the others' opposition or resistance. In other words both questions of organisational power and control, and other associated inequalities, are part of class relations and are what we mean by class structures.

It is for this reason — that work-based inequalities are a consequence of the class relationship which exists between employer and employees, and are thus an integral aspect of control relationships between these categories — that we now turn to a consideration of the inequalities of working life. Within sociology, conventionally, the exploration of work inequalities has been organised in terms of class analysis.

There are a number of elements in this. In the first place, class itself is often held to consist of variations in working conditions and the distribution of work-based rewards, among other factors. Thus Goldthorpe *et al.* in their exploration of postulated changes in the British class structure distinguish between economic, normative and relational changes. The last two need not concern us here; the first concerns us greatly. It refers to the 'experience of work' — to a consideration of the worker as a producer, and the experiences which follow from this basic role. In operational terms Goldthorpe *et al.* define this role in terms of: level of job satisfaction; level of skill, work stresses and deprivations; work conditions and arrangements and opportunities for promotion. (Goldthorpe *et al.* 1969.)

Secondly, these work-based inequalities, which are regarded as the basis of class differences, are also employed as evidence for the existence and persistence of class boundaries. Although, as we shall see, class itself can be defined in a more theoretical way — in terms, for example, of ownership or non-ownership of the means of production — it is usual for such definitions to be operationalised in terms of empirical inequalities in the distribution of work rewards and deprivations. Wedderburn and Craig (1974, p. 141) note for example that these work-based class inequalities tend to cluster together with a (relatively) deprived position on one scale coinciding with a low position on another. Furthermore the overall pattern of distribution remains remarkably persistent over time.

Conventional sociological analyses of work-based inequalities regard these inequalities as (a) evidence of class differences, (b) the basis for the location – or legitimation – of class boundaries, and (c) playing some part in the development of distinctive class images, and thus of distinctive class attitudes and political action. Our analysis in this chapter will broadly conform with this tradition. Like earlier writers we seek to document the major axes of work inequality and the major differences that occur along these axes. But we shall attempt more than this. We shall also seek to explain these inequalities in terms of the interplay of basic class forces and of the relationship between capital and labour. The theme of this book is the relationship between work inequalities and work experiences, and the structural dynamics of capitalist economies. We seek to identify the basic forces and contradictions of such economies and relate these to the principles (and apparent confusions over) work design criteria, control structures and methods. Behind these we shall identify the interplay of class relationships.

Thus we are using class in two connected but distinct ways. On the one hand we are using it to describe and organise existing empirical inequalities. On the other, we are using it to describe the basic relationship between capital and labour which generates both the inequalities described below, and the need for control and regulation described in later chapters. Furthermore, class inequalities and the need for control are themselves related in that the former supply a constant potential basis for both employee resistance and the definition of control, and management power, as illegitimate or even immoral. The following two chapters will attempt to relate class relationships and class struggle, within the context of management's need to achieve profitability, to managerial strategies of work design and work control. But first we must document some of the more significant and obvious work-based inequalities.

Differences in pay, conditions and prospects

Routh's historical survey of pay differences shows a striking continuity of relative pay differences. Table 1 shows some of the differences between manual and non-manual workers, and between men and women. These figures support the following comment from a *New Society* report of 1979: 'The workplace has traditionally been divided into two camps: the blue versus the white collar worker.... The most obvious disparity between manual and non-manual workers lies in the size and composition of pay packets. In April 1978, male full-time manual workers aged 21 and over earned on average a gross weekly wage of £80.70 compared with an average of £100.70 for white collar males...

The proportionate disparities have not altered much since the 1880s, although the differentials have narrowed slightly during the seventies.' (1979, p. 302.)

Table 1 *Distribution of income, 1982* (gross weekly earnings)

	Male (aged 21 and over)			Female (aged 18 and over)		
	Manual	Non Man	All	Manual	Non Man	All
10% earn less than	£ 85.5	£ 98.9	£ 89.7	£ 53	£ 63.4	£ 60.2
25% earn less than	£102.4	£125.4	£109.9	£ 62.8	£ 75.9	£ 71.7
50% earn less than	£125.2	£162.5	£139.1	£ 76.7	£ 95.6	£ 90
25% earn more than	£154.6	£210.5	£180.5	£ 92.4	£124.7	£116.5
10% earn more than	£191	£275.2	£233.8	£110.5	£158.8	£152

Source: *New Earnings Survey,* 1982
Note: Tables 1-4 refer to full time workers in all industries and services, excluding those whose pay was affected by absence.

There are also significant variations between pay levels of male and female workers, as Table 1 shows. In a study in the late sixties it was noted that out of 32 industries in the lowest quartile of the earnings distribution, half were in the highest quartile of the distribution by the proportion of women employed. In other words, industries employing most women were the worst paid industries (Marquand, 1967). Table 2 shows the relationship between women's pay levels and those of men. The best paid manual women (who constitute a minority among working women) receive only 71% of the average male wage. Jackson (1976) argues that this difference is a result of three factors: women are concentrated in poorly paid industries and in less skilled and therefore less well paid work; they are paid less for the same work when they manage to find it; and they tend to work fewer hours than men, mainly because they do not do so much overtime. Table 3 supports this.

Table 2 *Women's wages as percentage of males', 1970-82* (average gross hourly earnings, excluding overtime)

1970	1975	1976	1977	1978	1979	1980	1981	1982
63.1	72.1	75.1	75.5	73.9	73.0	73.5	74.8	73.9

Source: *New Earnings Survey,* 1982
Note: Refers to workers aged 18 and over.

Table 3 *Weekly Earnings of Manual Workers Compared with Non Manual, 1982*

	Male (aged 21 and over)			Female (aged 18 and over)		
	Weekly in £	*As % of Av.*	*Hours Worked*	*Weekly in £*	*As % of Av.*	*Hours Worked*
All	£154.5	100	41.7	£ 99	100	37.1
Manual	£133.8	87	44.3	£ 80.1	81	39.3
Non Man	£178.9	116	38.2	£104.9	106	36.5

Source: *Employment Gazette,* Nov. 1982

Table 3 shows that differences between men's and women's wage rates are related to differences in hours worked. Table 2 shows women's pay as a percentage of men's over the last 12 years. In 1982 it was 73.9% of men's pay.

Differences in level of pay are clearly not all the story. Working class workers must work for more hours in order to achieve a given level of income. As Goldthorpe *et al.* in their classic study of work inequalities noted, '... in order to gain parity in earnings with their fellow employees in clerical grades the shop floor men we studied might have to work up to 25% longer.' (Goldthorpe *et al.* 1969, p. 61.) Table 3 shows the extent of these variations. And Table 4 charts the amount of overtime worked by employees of different classes and by sex, as well as giving the proportion of income represented by overtime payments. For male manual workers 24% of weekly wage is derived from variable and fluctuating elements such as overtime and bonus payments.

Table 4 *Overtime, Shift and PBR Payments, 1982*

	Amount O/T in hours	*Weekly earnings from O/T, PBR etc. in £*	*O/T etc. payments as proportion of weekly wage*
All males	3.3	£21.1	14%
Manual male	4.9	£31.9	24%
Non manual males	1.2	£10.5	6%
All females	0.5	£ 5.1	5%
Manual females	1.0	£ 9.3	13%
Non manual females	0.4	£ 3.5	3%

Source: *New Earnings Survey,* 1982

Notes: (i) PBR — Payment by results schemes, including various piecework and bonus systems. (ii) Table refers to men aged 21 and over, and women aged 18 and over.

Table 4 adds further information on the differences in hours worked between male manual and non-manual workers. A particularly important class implication of such differences is not only that manual workers must sacrifice more of their time in order to achieve their income, but also that in times of recession it is precisely this sort of overtime work which is most vulnerable, thus making workers who rely on it for a considerable proportion of their weekly wage, as many clearly do, particularly likely to suffer financial loss.

Differences in level of pay, and the number of hours necessary to achieve it, are compounded by differences in job prospects. A 1973 study from the Office of Manpower Economics showed that only 3% of manual workers were paid on incremental scales, compared with 90% of white collar workers. Manual workers reach their wage peak in their forties and stay at that level during their fifties.

The vast majority of manual jobs offer no annual increments, and no opportunities for progression. Taylor (1982) quotes two contributors to the Royal Commission on the Distribution of Wealth and Income as reporting that: 'No manual jobs offer much prospect of real wage increases (other than from economic growth) after the first ten years. So in a sense more than half of the labour force are in jobs without prospects.' (Royal Commission on the Distribution of Income and Wealth, Background Paper No. 5, 1978, p. 51.)

Inequalities in rewards can be seen at their extreme by comparing senior management salaries with those of shop-floor workers, but such figures are not very meaningful in themselves because salary figures tell us nothing about the non-wage benefits received by top managers. It is only takeovers and boardroom disputes that force such facts out into the open. For example, in 1981 when the Swedish Esselte group tried to take over the British firm Letraset, the chairman of the latter had a net salary of £67,200 per year. But this salary figure ignored other parts of the remuneration package which included a rent-free company house, two company cars plus driver and a guaranteed pension of £40,000 p.a. at 60 years of age. The total package was estimated to be worth £195,000 p.a.; in other words nearly *three times* the quoted salary (*The Standard,* 12 Oct. 1981). That this example is not a peculiar one is indicated by a survey of 224 companies conducted by a firm of management consultants. This showed that the average cost of providing benefits, primarily to white-collar staff, was one-quarter of payroll, and for two companies it was 50% of payroll (Hay-MSL, 1979).

Job content, and skill levels

Another major area of inequality is in the nature of the work itself. It is of course difficult to measure quantitatively differences in work-based creativity, boredom, autonomy, routine. There are highly important and obvious differences between the work of a company director and that of a bus driver or office worker or factory worker But these differences are difficult to measure. Nevertheless a considerable amount of information can be gathered about the content of jobs. One source of information is workers' attitudes. All things being equal it is probably safe to say that differences in skill and creativity are significantly related to workers' attitudes towards their work, and particularly to their (hypothetical) propensity to take the same job again if they were able to start their work lives anew. Numerous studies have catalogued the major variations between class groups which emerge in response to questions like these. For example, on the basis of their research, Goldthorpe and his colleagues report: 'So far therefore as their typical work experience is concerned, the industrial workers in our sample are still, we would argue, quite significantly differentiated from most varieties of white-collar man: this experience involves stresses and deprivations that are not usually met in white-collar occupations and is, on the other hand, much less likely to comprise elements that are inherently rewarding.' (Goldthorpe *et al.* 1969, p. 63.) Furthermore, these authors report that the reasons the workers studied gave for liking their jobs were, overwhelmingly, to do not with the content of the work — for there was minimal basis for any intrinsic satisfaction — but with the high level of pay that could be earned (with overtime, of course). At the same time the proportion of respondents who stated that they found their repetitive, fragmented and rationalised jobs monotonous, unable to absorb their attention and excessively fast, was very high.

Numerous writers have found a relationship between skill and satisfaction, and have noted the highly unequal distribution of skill. The most highly satisfied workers are the ones with the most task discretion — professionals and businessmen. Within factories, satisfaction/skill are more prevalent among white-collar workers than on the shop floor. Within working class groups, satisfaction is highest among the skilled craftsmen (Blauner, 1960, p. 475). Among middle class jobs — the 'high discretion' roles described so usefully by Alan Fox — it is quite usual for jobs to be invested not only with skill and responsibility, but with discretion, under the assumption that these jobs cannot be broken down and bureaucratised to the same degree as lower level jobs. But 'low-discretion' work contains five inter-related features. First, the worker perceives his superiors behaving as if he/she cannot be trusted to deliver the desired work performance. Second, workers are closely supervised. Thirdly, each worker's activities are closely coordinated with the work of others. Fourthly, any mistakes are held to be the consequence of worker indifference or carelessness. Finally, any conflicts that occur are regarded as structural, and form the basis of bargaining between opposed groups.

Empirical support for this assessment can be found in numerous studies. For example, Davis *et al.*, on the basis of a study of job design criteria conducted in the 1950s, conclude that 'job design practices are consistent with the principles of rationalisation or scientific management. They minimise the dependence of the organisation on the individual. At the same time they minimise the contribution of the individual to the work of the organisation, i.e. its production process...job design practices minimise the effects of the individual's actions on the organisation...by specifying jobs requiring short training time and having low skill requirements.' (Davis *et al.* 1972, pp. 80-1.)

A more recent study by Taylor (1979), of engineers and systems analysts as job designers, shows a continuing pattern:

> ...twenty years of technological progress and innovation have had little corresponding effect on the professional values of design practitioners... production engineers and systems analysts select job design criteria remarkably similar to those chosen by their predecessors in the 1950s. They still prefer to minimize the immediate costs of production rather than to emphasize a long-term approach to job design which recognizes the economic cost of worker frustration and acknowledges employee satisfaction and motivation. (p. 61.)

Blackburn and Mann, in an important empirical investigation of skill differences in a sample of firms in the Peterborough area, report that by assessing skill components in terms of certain job requirements (mathematical calculation, complexity of decisions etc.) they consistently found themselves giving high scores to driving jobs. Yet these are not usually regarded as highly skilled by job evaluation schemes within industry. Nevertheless in terms of purely technical criteria, these jobs were amongst the most skilled they encountered and only 13% of the sample of jobs required greater skill than driving. The authors' conclusion is depressing indeed: 87% of the workers studied '...exercise less skill at work than they would if they drove to work. Indeed most of them expend more mental effort and resourcefulness in getting to work than in doing their jobs.' (Blackburn and Mann, 1979, p. 280). And this with a sample of jobs which had been deliberately widened beyond the confines of typical factory jobs. 'And yet we still confirm the traditional picture of monotonous jobs, debased skills and the under-use of human capacities. We must therefore conclude that this is indeed the objective situation of the majority of the manual working class.' (Blackburn and Mann, 1979, p. 102.)

Once again there are differences in the distribution of skilled work and creative work, on gender and racial lines. Prandy (1979) reports that 'A smaller proportion of them [immigrants] secure non-manual occupations and, of those doing manual work, fewer are employed in skilled jobs or in supervisory positions.' (Prandy, 1979, p. 71.)

We have seen that the typical low paid worker is female. In general women outnumber men in the low paid sector by more than 5 to 1. But women's work is not only poorly paid; it is also usually less skilled and more arduous. In 1980 some 74% of women worked in only five occupational groups – typists/secretaries; maids and related service work; nurses; canteen assistants and sewing machinists. Even in offices where women hold three-quarters of available jobs, they hold less than one fifth of management posts.

It is difficult to find statistical indices of skill; work satisfaction surveys, although they might to the uninitiated seem to measure skill level, in fact seem to tap levels of fatalism and acceptance. Length of training is probably a reasonable index of skill however and Table 5 shows differences on a gender basis between percentages of men and women workers who have had different amounts of training.

Table 5 *Training at first job undertaken by 16-17 year olds*
Table shows % of workers who have had different amounts of training.

	Male	Female
Nil	31.1	42.2
1-2 weeks	3.0	4.6
3-8 weeks	9.9	21.5
9-26 weeks	10.3	17.0
27-52 weeks	3.5	3.8
53-104 weeks	6.1	4.5
105 + weeks	36.2	6.5

Source: *Careers Office Survey,* 1978

Exposure to work-based accidents and disease

The workplace can be highly dangerous. But two points must be made about such dangers, whether they originate in accidents, risk of exposure to radioactivity, carcinogenic substances, poisonous dusts or whatever. The first is that such dangers, like so many features of work, are not distributed evenly. Despite the publicity surrounding managerial stress and executive disorders – psychosomatic complaints, cardio-vascular diseases and intestinal and gastric conditions which are associated with such stress – the realities of the distribution of work-related accidents and disease show that they are most prevalent among manual workers. Tables 6 and 7 show the class dimension of illness. As Taylor reports, the official statistics from the Factory Inspectorate do suggest a fall in the number of deaths and accidents at work (Taylor, 1982, p. 133). But what is more important for our purposes is the fact that of these, nearly all work deaths resulting from accidents at work are among manual workers. In 1980, 366 people died as a result of accidents at work. Many more of course were injured (208,053) or were afflicted by work-related disease (11,573 in 1979). In 1979, over 400 death certificates were issued which mentioned asbestos-related disease. And in 1978, 36,000 people received compensation for pneumoconiosis. The vast majority of these work-related accidents and diseases occurred among manual workers, for the obvious reason that exposure to dangerous processes, conditions or substances is far, far more likely among working class jobs than in office or management work. Often workers on the shop floor have no knowledge of the risks they are running. For example in 1970 Bob Smith, a worker at a London asbestos factory, was given just eight years to live. He died in August 1973, a victim of asbestosis. Before he died, he said:

We've all got to go sometime. It's just that I know I'm going to go sooner than I should be going. I'm not afraid of it. But the knowledge is there, that you're going to go before your time, through no fault of your own. I feel very bitter about it because, if they'd told me of the dangers, I wouldn't be in the position I'm in. Really and truly, they should have told me. They knew.

The Listener, 2 May 1974.

Furthermore, this unequal distribution of work-related illness and accidents is not the result simply of the utilisation of modern technology and work systems, or of the inevitable dangers associated with inherently risky enterprises – mining or deep-sea fishing. Nor are these figures the consequences of worker indifference or carelessness. They, and the numerous individual cases of suffering and premature death which they coldly represent, are the systematic outcome of the values and pressures of production.

Table 6 *Sickness: class differences   (a) in early adulthood, 15 to 44* (rates per 1000 population)

Socio-economic group	Long-standing illness		Restricted activity		Consultation	
	Men	Women	Men	Women	Men	Women
Professional	145.4	138.2	84.0	106.4	75.5	140.4
Managerial	149.7	141.9	63.1	93.3	61.3	133.9
Intermediate	164.0	145.4	85.1	105.5	72.3	130.6
Skilled manual	161.9	167.2	89.7	95.2	85.1	142.5
Semi-skilled manual	173.8	170.3	81.5	99.3	80.5	146.0
Unskilled manual	197.4	202.3	110.4	95.3	93.5	145.9

Source: General Household Surveys 1974-6 from 'Inequalities in Health', DHSS, 1980, p. 52.

Table 7 *Sickness: class differences   (b) middle age, 45 to 64* (rates per 1000 population)

Socio-economic group	Long-standing illness		Restricted activity		Consultation	
	Men	Women	Men	Women	Men	Women
Professional	228.9	291.3	71.1	92.2	75.6	94.7
Managerial	257.0	265.7	75.4	77.0	74.8	99.8
Intermediate	368.0	329.7	98.4	94.6	122.1	122.4
Skilled manual	357.7	315.1	102.6	102.7	112.4	109.2
Semi-skilled manual	387.6	380.8	101.0	114.9	124.9	121.5
Unskilled manual	485.5	401.6	120.0	111.9	145.5	122.6

Source: From 'Inequalities in Health', DHSS, 1980, p. 53.

But to call these accidents unpredictable can be misleading. In many cases they are systematic products of the value placed, in work and production, on quantity of production, speed of work, profitability of technique, rather than on human life and health. Numerous commentators have made this point. 'Accidents' at work – and work-based diseases – do not simply happen, they occur as a result of work priorities and objectives and the low level of importance allocated (in practice if not in rhetoric) to employees' safety.

A further indication of the structural origin of these appalling figures can be gathered when one considers the absurd undermanning of the Factory Inspectorate – just over one thousand inspectors to cope with over 1¾ million work establishments in 1971 (Nichols and Armstrong, 1973, pp. 1-2); the procedures whereby owners of workplaces are notified in advance of a planned visit; the fact that many accidents are not notified to the inspectorate at all; the inspectorate's unwillingness to take cases to court, and the derisory fines which are imposed when an employer is found guilty of negligence (Nichols and Armstrong report that the average fine in 1971 was £40) – all support these authors' conclusions that safety at work simply is not taken seriously. What is taken seriously of course is profit, production, output. And numerous participant researchers have suggested that management at least is quite clear about the relative importance of safety or profit. Göran Palm, for example, reports that '... accidents and near-accidents generally precede the safety measures. Someone falls down steep stairs first, and then the stairs are made less steep. Someone crushes a finger when he lifts something, and then a lifting machine is purchased. Week after week and year after year the industrial safety officers present their demands for safety devices, enclosures of machinery and rebuilding operations of various types but at least one good near-accident is required before anything is done and not merely promised. It is as though management first needed tragic and palpable proof that the safety measure is justified.' (Palm, 1977, pp. 22-3.)

There are also significant differences between manual and non-manual jobs in the extent and nature of provision that is supplied by the employer in the case of illness or accident. Table 8 demonstrates the variation in percentages of various occupational categories who continue to be paid during sickness, and who are covered by private pension schemes. Table 9 shows class variations in the length of time that must be worked before employees of different sorts qualify for sick pay, and Table 10 shows variation in the maximum duration of sick pay entitlement. A similar situation exists with regard to the provision of pensions, where inequalities in retirement mirror those of work life (see Taylor, 1982, pp. 140-1).

Table 8 *Persons covered by employers' sick pay and pension arrangements by socio-economic group, 1971-1979*
Full-time employees aged 16 or over in Great Britain

Socio-Economic Group*	Get paid when sick		Covered by private pension scheme	
	1971 %	1976 %	1975 %	1979 %
Managers in large establishments	98	97	87	88
Managers in small establishments	93	86	51	60
Professional workers – employees	99	96	82	82
Intermediate Non-manual	90	95	82	86
Junior non-manual	79	88	58	63
Personal service workers	49	65	35	37
Foreman and supervisors	77	80	71	71
Skilled manual workers	47	56	51	56
Semi-skilled manual workers	45	56	48	57
Unskilled manual workers	49	57	41	56
Agricultural workers	58	67	22	21
Average all groups	65	74	58	64

*Figures for farm managers excluded due to small numbers; figures for those in the Armed Forces are excluded.
Source: General Household Survey, 1971, 1975, 1976, 1979.

Table 9 *Qualifying period before sick pay paid, 1974*

Percentage of each group required to work following amounts of time

	None	6 months	1 year	Not known
Manual male	28.4	23.3	25.9	22.4
Non manual male	67.1	14.1	5.7	13.1
Manual female	23.8	33.1	19.9	23.2
Non manual female	65.1	14.5	6.2	14.2

Source: DHSS 1977, *Survey of Occupational and Sick Schemes*. Sample of 7000 manufacturing and service employers.

Table 10 *Maximum duration of sick pay entitlement, 1974*

Percentages of workers entitled to sick pay for periods of

	Up to 4 weeks	5-12 weeks	13-26 weeks	27-51 weeks	52 ± weeks	Discretionary
Manual male	27.1	17.9	27.1	6.2	15.0	6.4
Non manual male	11.4	12.0	23.1	9.7	26.7	16.9
Manual female	36.1	15.5	22.8	7.2	12.2	6.3
Non manual female	21.7	16.9	21.8	10.7	17.6	11.2

Source: DHSS 1977

Job security and unemployment

Not only are the deprivations and dangers of work distributed unequally, as we have noted, but so are the security of work itself, and the risk of unemployment or redundancy.

Unemployment has a number of direct and costly implications for the individual. The most obvious and pressing is the financial cost. Certainly unemployment benefit has improved since the forties. In 1948, National Assistance paid to a man with two young children represented less than half the net earnings of the average male earner. In 1977, the supplementary benefit such a man would receive would be more than 66%. Nevertheless, this still represents a very considerable reduction in weekly earnings (Deacon, 1981, p. 82).

However, the major cost of unemployment is probably personal, and a major element in it is the loss of the value and dignity which are attached to work and work identities. To lose one's job in a society where individual worth is largely established through work and through earning power is to run the risk of being regarded as worthless. This definition is amplified by the tendency to relate unemployment to the moral and personal responsibility of the unemployed individual. The recent enormous increase in unemployment has, as might have been expected, been accompanied by arguments that many of those who are unemployed are so because of their own inadequacy – that they are unemployable – and that unemployment benefits are over-generous and reduce incentives for the 'workshy'; and that some of the unemployed are so only because they refuse to look, or to move, for work (Deacon, 1981, p. 59).

Recently unemployment has risen to levels which earlier would have been politically unacceptable. As Deacon notes, the White Paper on Employment Policy published by the Coalition Government of June 1944 began: 'The Government accepts as one of their primary aims and responsibilities the maintenance of a high and stable level of employment after the war.' (Deacon, 1981, p. 59.) But such sentiments had been forgotten by the time the monetarist government of Mrs Thatcher took office in the late 'seventies. That government defined its major mission as the defeat not of unemployment but of inflation; and acknowledged that this campaign might well have an entirely unavoidable and necessary consequence for the level of unemployment. Politically, unemployment is now defined not as a symptom of government callousness or policy (or incompetence), but of national and individual sloth and greed. This conveniently locates responsibility for unemployment levels outside the government.

Like other costs associated with work, unemployment, and the risk of unemployment, are distributed unequally. Some members of the workforce are much more likely to be made unemployed than others. And some people are made unemployed more frequently than others. If unemployment were shared out equally, it has been calculated that everyone would be out of work every six years, or eight spells in a work life. But in fact, in 1979, just 3% of the workforce was bearing 70% of the total weeks of unemployment in a year (Metcalf, 1980, p. 24, quoted in Sinfield, 1981, p. 18).

Furthermore those most likely to be made unemployed are those who are most disadvantaged at work: those in the poorest jobs, low-paying insecure occupations; the youngest, or oldest workers; women; members of minority racial groups. 'Unemployment strikes, and strikes most harshly and frequently, those who are among the poorest and least powerful in the labour force and in society as a whole.' (Sinfield, 1981 pp. 18-19.) The burden of unemployment tends to fall particularly frequently on racial minorities. All the available data consistently show a higher level of unemployment among ethnic minority groups, which is not attributable solely to their young age structures. For example, a survey of a matched (by sex, educational qualifications and labour market area) group of young West Indians and whites in London and Birmingham, showed that during the five years of the survey, 47.2% of the West Indians but only 32.8% of the whites experienced at least one dismissal or redundancy. Furthermore, the average duration of unemployment for the whites was about 13 weeks compared with nearly 25 weeks for the West Indians (Dex, 1983, pp.44-5). The sample size was small — 166 young male workers — but the results are significantly different and worse for the minority group.

Conclusions

Our first chapter has documented the major forms of work-based inequalities. We have presented this information for a number of related reasons. First, we feel that no understanding of what work is like — of the 'quality of working life' — is possible without some consideration of the most basic feature of work: that it is a crucial source of variations in peoples' 'life chances'. Those events in our lives which importantly affect our health, happiness, sense of well-being, material comfort, freedom from anxiety — derive from our work. And work is above all a place, and a source of inequality.

For many writers the distribution of work-based rewards and deprivation is the basic ingredient in class differences. We accept this, but wish to use the concept of class to do more than merely document what are regarded as class differences in the distribution of life chances. We wish also to use class as a way of understanding the basic relationship between classes which gives rise to the inequalities described above. In other words the inequalities depicted here arise because of a basic conflict of interest between classes, and the relative power of each class to defend or improve its position. Later chapters of the book will explore the role of class relations in the development of control strategies and contradictions, the design of work and the design of technology.

A major focus of this book is on the conflict between class relations — between classes opposed to each other, each trying to improve its position — and organisational relations. Of course the latter are examples of the former. But equally clearly in most cases, most of the time, actual relationships within the enterprise do not even approximate to the degree of overt conflict one might expect from a purely theoretical analysis of class relationships. In fact such a coincidence of class relations with organisational relations would hardly be possible; the enterprise could not operate on the basis of overt, actual conflict between management and workers. We are concerned to explore the origins and implications of precisely this paradox: that if organisational relationships are a version of class relations, they somehow manage to develop features which effectively deny and disguise this connection to most of those concerned, or they recognise the connection but define it in ways which can be incorporated into organisational life. What is it, then about organisational strategy, control methods, and work design principles which enables them at one and the same time to advance class interests, to support class differences of the sort described earlier, and yet at the same time to deny class interests and differences?

How is it possible for one class to differ in 'life chances' from another class as strikingly as we have documented, and for it to control and organise the work of that relatively deprived class, and yet for this class relationship to persist relatively unquestioned? It is to these issues and their implications that we now turn.

3 · The Social Organisation of Work

Chapter 2 established our basic premise: that the individual experience of work, with all the problems this can bring, was structured and patterned in ways which could be described in terms of class structuring, and that these patterns of experience, deprivation and opportunity were themselves the systematic product of economic and social processes. It is not enough merely to describe the patterning of the highly unequal distribution of work rewards and deprivations, we must also seek to understand and explain these phenomena by reference to underlying social and economic processes. Such is the objective of this chapter.

Evolution of monopoly capitalism

We have noted that the basic capitalist dynamic which organises the design of work, the nature and direction of investment, the structuring of large-scale organisations, the search for new products, markets and technologies, is the search for profit. Under capitalism, work is organised to achieve a level of profit sufficient not only to remunerate the owners of capital, and ensure that capital is not transferred elsewhere, or put to other uses, but also to ensure a constant process of re-investment in new technologies, markets, products, and work systems, so that the firm is constantly improving its competitiveness. The process goes like this: 'Competition inexorably pushes firms to seek out new ways to gain an edge, to recapture old markets and conquer new ones. Not only are old technologies and practices stretched to their limits, but capitalists constantly search for new productive methods. In the economist's language, entrepreneurs expand production out along their cost curves, but competition robs them of their expected profits. The entrepreneurs are thus driven to reinvest profits or borrow more funds, hoping that innovation or expansion will lower their entire cost curves and thereby reclaim the lost margins. But soon their competitors will also adopt any innovations and prices will decline to reflect that event. Once again, the stage is set for a new competition, this time with fewer competitors surviving to fight the next battle, a battle to be waged on a much grander scale.' (Edwards, 1979, pp. 39-40.)

This is the natural order of things – the 'facts of life' – under capitalism. The imperative for firms to accumulate has urgent implications for the nature and distribution of the inequalities of working life. But the requirement for firms to compete to survive, and thus to accumulate capital for further investment, is exacerbated by the chronic instability of capitalism. The development of new technologies — of fundamental revolutions in technology — leads to a transformation of the whole productive technology of the economy, and thus to increased profitability. But the gradual spread of the new technology must lead after a sustained phase of accelerated accumulation, to a prolonged phase of decelerating accumulation, i.e. renewed under-investment and the reappearance of idle capital. Each of the cyclical movements which characterise the history of capitalism contains the same essential elements: an initial phase distinguished by technological innovation when accumulation, growth and profit rates accelerate; and a secondary and related phase when profits decline, and accumulation decelerates. Once profits begin to decline, investment falls, and managers prefer cost-reducing rationalisation and invention, aiming for the re-achievement of a satisfactory level of profits through attacks on the working class and attempts to reduce the cost of labour.

Since the late sixties the capitalist world has been experiencing a particular, and well-documented, form of crisis. Initially during the sixties the problem was one of over-accumulation in relation to labour supply, with a consequent fall in profitability, as Table 1 illustrates.

Table 1 *Rates of profit for industrial & commercial companies, 1960-75*

	Percentages before tax				
	1960	*1965*	*1970*	*1973*	*1975*
UK	14.2	11.8	8.7	7.2	3.5
USA	9.9	13.7	8.1	8.6	6.9
France	11.9	9.9	11.1	10.2	4.1
Japan	19.7	15.3	22.7	14.7	9.5

Source: Glyn & Harrison (1980), p. 12.

The tendency indicated by Table 1 was considerably accelerated by the success of organised labour during this period to achieve some increases in real wages. One result of the coincidence of labour shortages, the rise in real wages, and the attempts by firms to continue to accumulate was rising levels of inflation, as firms marked up prices to maintain profits. Government responses to inflation took two forms — attacks on wages through various forms of wage control, social contract, wage freeze, etc., — and measures of economic policy which attempted to control money supply and reduce demand.

By the 1980s the problem of the UK, and to a lesser but still serious degree, of capitalism as a whole, was clear: stagnation. Profits declined drastically, falling by the mid-seventies in the UK, France and Italy, to less than one third of the level of the early sixties (McCracken, 1977). Production was down – by 1979, down by 18% of the level of 1963-73. Unemployment was up – by 1979, by about 10 million in the capitalist world compared to sixties levels. And investment was down – down to three quarters of the level which would have been reached if pre-1973 levels had been maintained (Glyn and Harrison, 1980, p. 25). An important factor in this stagnation, particularly as it affected the UK economy, was the relative power of the working class (at least up to 1979) to resist the exacerbation of its exploitation: 'Britain became the only imperialist power which proved unable to increase the rate of exploitation of its working class significantly during or after the Second World War. ... From a capitalist point of view the result was evident: an erosion of the rate of profit, and a much slower rate of economic growth and accumulation than in the other imperialist countries.' (Mandel, 1978, p. 179.)

Mandel's assessment establishes that under conditions of deep economic crisis, Marx's analysis of the role of labour/capital conflict in establishing the precise level of profitability explains why a major capitalist and governmental response will be various forms of attack on labour power and attempts to cheapen labour. We shall be able to assess the applicability of these likely outcomes as we proceed with our analysis of the nature and extent of work inequalities, for throughout this analysis two major questions should be borne in mind: what are the origins of these variations, these inequalities (or, how do these relate to the basic dynamics of the society and the economy?), and what impact do these highly differential experiences have on the formation and consciousness of group resistance and organisation? We shall return to these questions frequently.

At this stage, the major determining factor should be clear: capitalism depends upon constant pressure on firms to compete, to accumulate, to reinvest. Firms must compete to survive, but competition is, at least in some areas, increasingly fierce; firms must be profitable to compete, but profits are falling. What effects will these basic difficulties have on the development of the characteristic employing organisation in this phase of capitalist development? And what strategies and options are open to, and preferred by, the owners and controllers of such organisations under these difficult conditions? The remainder of this chapter is devoted to a consideration of these questions.

The first point to make concerns the organisation of capitalism in its 'late' or 'monopoly' phase. Capitalism at this stage demonstrates two key inter-related features: firstly, the institutionalisation of processes of capitalist control, ownership and decision-making, such that these processes, once the preserve of individual owners or senior managers, are now specialised and handled by expert departments or agencies according to elaborate, rational criteria. The functions of capital have thus become differentiated (ownership from control; aspects of control from each other, etc.) and removed from the personal competence of individuals. Internally, within the enterprise, functions have been separated and bureaucratised. Externally, the enterprise, now publicly-owned, (ownership itself is now differentiated) is locked into an elaborate and constraining series of relationships with financial institutions, expert agencies and government bodies. These large firms are usually highly diversified, with a large range of products, and a multi-divisional structure which has often grown through takeovers. A major trend in advanced industrial capitalism has been towards the concentration of more and more areas of economic activity in the hands of the large multi-divisional corporations (Chandler, 1977; Scott, 1979).

Secondly, the nature of the average enterprise has changed: a process of monopolisation has occurred. Through competition, many firms have found it harder and harder to survive while even larger firms have managed to gain large shares of the market, and thus monopolistic profits. Heilbroner reports that in the USA in 1968, the largest 100 firms controlled as great a proportion of corporate assets as did the top 200 in 1941 (Heilbroner, quoted in Nichols, 1980, p. 29). In Britain the 100 largest firms in 1970 produced about 40% of manufacturing net output, against 16% of output in 1909. Prais makes the further point that the growth of large firms is directly related to the role of financial institutions: 'The vast funds placed at the disposal of...institutional intermediaries, by being invested preferentially in large quoted companies, have contributed to financial pressures which have encouraged the formation of large industrial groups.' (Prais, 1976, p. 135.)

Table 2 *Enterprise size in manufacturing 1958-1978*

Enterprise size (number of employees)		2,000 and over	5,000 and over	10,000 and over	20,000 and over	50,000 and over
Number of	1958	469	180	74	32	8
enterprises	1978	428	179	83	37	10
Percentage of employees working for	1958	45.8	34.3	25.0	17.3	7.3
these enterprises	1978	56.2	44.6	34.6	25.0	12.5

Sources: (1958) *Historical Record of the Census of Production 1907-1970*, HMSO, 1978, Table 10. (1978) *Report of the 1978 Census of Production*, PA 1002, HMSO, 1981, Table 12.

With reference to the scale of employment of these large firms, it has been calculated that in both the USA and UK, about 25% to 27% of employees are engaged in manufacturing enterprises with over 20,000 employees. Furthermore, in 1978 half the manufacturing labour force in the UK was employed in enterprises with over 3,000 employees. As Prais concludes, it appears that there is '...an important long-term tendency towards increasing concentration...inherent in our economic system' (Prais, 1976, p. 167.) (See Table 2.)

There is a close relationship between the evolution of large firms, the institutionalisation and differentiation of internal control processes, and the development and role of external financial agencies. As Scott remarks: 'The massive growth of "institutional" shareholdings is thrusting the insurance companies, pension funds, banks etc., into positions of effective possession of industrial companies. These financial companies are themselves ...increasingly subject to impersonal possession. A complex system of intercorporate shareholdings and credit relations is emerging, within which particular corporations are controlled by the specific constellations of interest which have effective possession.' (Scott, 1979, p. 174.)

The characteristic enterprise within monopoly capitalism is highly differentiated functionally, is located within a complex and indispensable series of external financial arrangements and ties, and is increasingly large, in terms of numbers of employees, output and market share.

But what strategies and options are open to the owners/controllers of these large firms? And what impact may these strategies have on the inequalities of working life?

First, we must dispel any suggestion that the institutionalisation of capitalism, the depersonalisation and differentiation of capitalist functions, and the differentiation and dispersal of the ownership of the corporation, through public, joint-stock ownership, implies any radical alteration in the priority of profit and accumulation. The logic of the market for the modern, large-scale, monopolistic, financial-capital funded corporation is to cut costs in order to increase its share of the market. While the prevalence of monopolistic firms involves a reduction in the extent of competition (for there are now fewer competitors) it also involves an increase in the intensity of competition between the surviving enterprises. Moreover competition becomes increasingly international in form.

It has been suggested, in opposition to this view of the survival, indeed amplification, of the significance and urgency of profitability, that the emergence of the manager-controlled, publicly-owned enterprise signals the transition from the priority of profit, to the priority of more socially conscious objectives. In fact the emergence of institutional ownership and the dominance of financial organisations, if it signals any change in this respect, probably marks a move towards a more rational, purposive and efficient pursuit of the necessary objective of the capitalist enterprise: profit. All that has changed is the move towards long-term profit maximisation. As

Mandel notes, in monopolistic competition, 'Company strategy aims at long-term profit maximisation, in which factors such as domination of the market, share of the market, brand familiarity, future ability to meet demand, safeguarding of opportunities for innovation, i.e. for growth, become more important than the selling price which can be obtained immediately or the profit margin which this represents.' (Mandel 1972, p. 232.) In other words, the time-horizons of companies may change, but even large multi-nationals cannot bear substantial losses for more than three years running.

What then of the strategies and objectives of these firms under such conditions of declining profitability? As has been stressed, the corporation is still required to pursue long-term profit maximisation. This has direct implications for management/worker relations and for work organisation. The corporation's efforts to increase profitability – some of which are described below – may directly involve interventions in the class relations which exist between employers and employees. The search for profit inevitably occasions attempted alterations in the relative shares of profit and wages, and the wage/effort bargain. The organisation of the firm, and the strategies and objectives of the firm, must pertain to the balance of strength between capital and labour. This is the first, crucial point about corporate strategies: that despite rhetoric about efficiency and productivity and use of such neutral terms such as modernisation and rationalisation, they inevitably and centrally involve attempts to re-order class relations in terms which increase the relative advantage to capital, through manipulating the cost of a unit of labour, the relative size of profit.

Secondly, these corporate strategies not only reflect class relations between labour (wages) and capital (profit), they have a direct impact on levels of class consciousness, and thus on concrete class relationships. As Gintis has remarked, '....the profitability of production will depend intimately on the consciousness of workers...capital production will be organised not only to produce a marketable commodity but also to reproduce, from period to period, forms of worker consciousness compatible with future profits.' (Gintis, 1976, p. 42.) In other words the capitalist, in seeking to achieve profits, must also consider the forms and levels of consciousness of the employees (Littler and Salaman, 1982). To seek profits from alienated labour inevitably raises acute problems of control. The forms of corporate and state strategy described below all reflect the major priority of capital profit and the continued generation of profits. In so doing however, as will be discussed in Chapter 4, they also raise a series of major contradictions between mutually opposed tendencies – the need to specify and exploit versus the need to reproduce the conditions for this and further exploitation.

Those 'managerialist' writers who have used the dispersal of ownership as evidence of qualitative changes within the capitalist system ignore the fact that this, in as much as it has occurred, actually makes it easier for big stockholders, and institutions, to exercise a dominant influence on the corporation. The argument also overestimates the significance of individual motives in capitalist life. Capitalism does not depend on individual motivation – on the regular emergence, each generation, of a cohort of rapacious Gradgrinds. Capitalism creates its own systemic imperatives: be profitable, or go under. The emergence of new forms of financial organisation and control, the increasing concentration of production in ever larger units, the centralisation of money capital in ever larger financial units and the increasing depersonalisation and institutionalisation of capitalism itself represent not the transformation of capitalism but a key stage in its development (Scott, 1979).

We shall see that the organised, rationalised, specialised attempts by senior managers of large-scale corporations to ensure the profitability and efficiency of their corporations during a time of increasing competition and declining profitability have serious implications for the design of work and the nature and distribution of work inequalities. We shall consider these various strategies and implications under a number of discrete headings: work design and control within the corporation; the international movement of investment; and the state attack on organised labour.

Work design and control within the corporation

Numerous writers have noted that a major characteristic of the modern, large-scale, institutionalised corporation is the professionalisation and rationalisation of planning. Within the large corporation, decisions on products, markets, technologies, etc. have enormous financial implications, and once the early returns from technological innovations have declined drastically, profits are dependent on the ever more detailed and scrupulous planning of corporate decisions, and the elimination of waste and inefficiency. With profits declining, and competition mounting, every aspect of corporate functioning must be rigorously considered and evaluated. The function of such planning, as Galbraith and many others have noted, is to attempt to reduce or at least to foresee, the inherent uncertainty of the market. Mandel sees this as an 'inherent constraint' within late capitalism: '...to increase systematic control over all elements of the process of production, circulation and reproduction. ...' (Mandel, 1978, p. 240.) As we shall see, this constraint has numerous implications for corporate control over many aspects of corporate life and over the corporation's employees, and indeed for the concentration of state power over social and economic life. But the most significant aspect of the inherent constraint is that it requires tight control over wages and other costs, and also over all aspects of the development of the corporation's products and methods: research and innovation, materials, markets, technologies, investment decisions, forward planning and the basic decisions as to what, where, and how production will take place. Most of all, the 'inherent constraint' requires ever more and more corporate influence over the direction, quantity, quality, and intensity of workers' effort. Declining profitability, increasing competition and the overall requirement of general corporate planning and rationalisation requires greater control over work, not simply in order to increase levels of production, but to maximise the flexibility and efficiency of labour.

Each long wave of economic activity involves an expansion based on technological innovation and product improvement. Often indeed each wave is associated with a distinctive technological/product phase — nineteenth century engineering, early mid-twentieth century motor cars and aeroplanes, late twentieth century electronics — which is associated with a particular geographical location (UK, USA, Japan) and which, initially, gives its host economy an enormous lead. However, as innovations are disseminated, and as technological leads are reduced, profitability comes to depend on detailed improvements in techniques of production, on the smoothing out of the basic unchanged product design. Of particular significance during this phase, of embellishment rather than radical technical/product innovation, is the control and manipulation of labour.

But if the detailed and tightly specified control of labour becomes even more salient during periods of declining profitability (particularly in those economies which are still largely dependent on a now out-moded stage of technological development, with its associated products) it is not unequivocally clear just how the imperative to accumulate under these circumstances is translated into particular forms of labour/capital relations. A major contribution to this debate is that of Harry Braverman (1974), who argues that this imperative results in the increasing predominance of a particular form of work design — one which maximises the control of labour, while cheapening it and making it more transferable: the de-skilling of manual and office work, in accordance with the precepts of Taylorism or 'scientific management' — fragmentation of work, the reduction of jobs to minimal elements, the removal of all elements of discretion, etc. The issue of control at work is discussed in Chapter 4, and Taylorism is discussed in Chapter 5.

Capitalism under crisis then faces a major dilemma, and one which we shall find it necessary to treat on various occasions through the book, since it represents a major thrust and a major contradiction within current developments in work design and work organisation. The dilemma is an old one, recognised frequently by commentators and by managers themselves. Basically, it is this: the essential relations between capital and labour, occurring within the context of institutionalised competition, force the employer to seek increased control over the quantity and quality of workers' work efforts. Yet in so doing, relationships between employer and employees can so deteriorate as to lead to a further increase in control, surveillance, and specification, and a further withdrawal of commitment on the part of the work force. This deteriorating spiral of management/worker relations has been described by Fox (1974) and Gouldner (1954). As we shall see in Chapter 4, one way of viewing this dilemma is in terms of capital's simultaneous need for two distinct and occasionally opposed forms of control.

However, if a common response to the problems of profitability is to seek even tighter control over labour – increasing the specification of effort, and the quality of effort – such actions soon reveal a basic paradox: that the tighter the control of labour power, the more control is required. No degree of specification can ever remove the essential element of labour power: that it relies ultimately on the worker's willingness to co-operate. Short of removing the worker from the production process completely through automation and the use of robots – both increasingly popular options – the employer sooner or later is forced to seek to recover workers' willingness by harnessing their participation. Numerous management writers have described and extolled the Japanese system of management whereby workers' commitment is apparently achieved (with enviable consequences for productivity and quality) by delegating a degree of responsibility and quality control to the workers themselves (Cole, 1979; White and Trevor, 1983).

Productivity, writes Lester Thurow, can be made to 'bubble up' from the shop floor through changing organisational structure so that worker commitment is re-engaged. Taylorism is reaching a stage where its inherent logic is so plain, and so alienating, that it is becoming counter-productive: 'American firms are being run out of business not slowly, but quickly. General Motors is experimenting with small groups of workers – "quality control circles" – to control productivity, not because they like them but because they feel they must. If they don't do something new, they will be driven out of business.' (Thurow, 1981, p. 4.) Ford of Europe has recently been involved in similar experiments (see Chapter 5). As we shall see, the imperatives of accumulation, and the pressures of declining profitability, cause employers to place increased emphasis on the control and motivation of workers.

The international movement of capital

Increasing interest in the control of labour and its productivity is but one of a number of basic options open to the employer. As Mandel notes: 'Capital today has two ways available to it of reconstructing the industrial army: on the one hand, the intensification of capital exports and the systematic suffocation of investments at home, i.e. sending capital where there is still excess labour-power, instead of bringing labour-power to excess capital; on the other, the intensification of automation, or, in other words the concentration of investment to set free as much living labour as possible...' (Mandel, 1978, p. 182.)

Our first requirement is to plot the extent of this international movement of investment, then to see its implications for employment practices both in the base economies and those where the investment is placed. It is crucial to appreciate that in the last twenty years of the twentieth century we are dealing not simply with a world-wide structure of national economies, but with a world international economic system. We do not mean to imply by this that the world capitalist economy will be uniform, stable and even in its organisation. On the contrary, a major feature of this system is precisely that it is differentiated into areas of unequal development with central and peripheral areas and economies. Indeed one of the most significant features of the world capitalist economy is the nature of the relationship between centre and periphery, the industrialised West and many undeveloped, dependent economies. The international division of labour requires many societies to participate in the world order in ways which exclude many economies from the benefits enjoyed by the central, metropolitan economies. We follow Wallerstein in stressing the unity of the world economy, its lack of overarching political structure and its dependence on the 'market' as a basis for redistribution of surplus (Wallerstein, 1976, p. 348).

One of the major institutions of the world economy is the multinational company. If we define multinationals as companies with at least 25% of their turnover, investment, production or employment being generated outside their country of origin, then 75 to 85 of the 200 largest American and European companies fall in this category (Mandel, 1978, p. 321). In early 1972, '...the total turnover of all companies which have been described as multinational was estimated to be between 300 and 450 billion dollars...in other words, approximately 15%-20% of the gross social product of the whole capitalist world.' (Mandel, 1979, p. 322.) The development of multinational corporations, and the increasing tendency for these corporations to extend their operations overseas, reflects the fact that the internationalisation of production encourages the internationalisation of capital. An increasing proportion of international trade takes place within the same multinational company, as internal transfers. For example, many of the cars 'imported' into Britain represent the internal transactions of General Motors or Ford.

The multinational corporation becomes the typical characteristic form of economic organisation within late capitalism. Several pressures drive it to international investment: in a number of spheres merely local production is no longer sufficient in quantity to achieve acceptable levels of return on the amount of capital investment necessary; the limitation of sales in home markets drives companies to find markets outside the national boundaries; the increasing search for new products and high profits forces companies to establish international production for international markets; the existence of different tax laws, of different state policies for encouraging investment, of various forms of tariff restrictions and protectionist arrangements, encourages multi-nationals to locate production within potential market areas in order to avoid tariffs, or to take advantage of concessionary tax arrangements. As Frobel *et al.* demonstrate in their exhaustive survey of investment abroad by West German corporations, between 1961 and 1976 '...the number of foreign subsidiaries belonging to the companies surveyed...increased fourfold,...the number of employees abroad by these companies increased fivefold between 1961 and 1974.' (Frobel *et al.*, 1980, p. 21.) In some industries the proportion of investments going abroad is extraordinarily high. The authors calculate that in the first six months of 1976, as much as 70% of investment from the German electrical engineering industry went abroad.

If, as many authors now argue, the changing circumstances of world capitalism, and the search for profits, forces the characteristic modern capitalist enterprise to reorganise production internationally, what are the preconditions, and more importantly, the implications for work organisation and employment practices, of these developments? Can we find any connections between them and the constant struggle between capital and labour, with capital attempting to increase its control over the specification and quantity of worker effort, and over worker willingness, or acquiescence?

The major preconditions for the development of the international division of labour are straightforward: the development, or existence, of a world-wide reservoir of labour (which, as we shall see, represents a major attraction for foreign investment and production), the development of technology and work organisation such that the international fragmentation of production processes is possible, with the consequence that relatively untrained labour can be employed; and the development of technologies which make the actual location of production largely irrelevant to geographical distance – that is, communications and transport technologies.

The major advantages of locating production internationally are equally obvious. The increasing concentration by large-scale corporations within the home economies, on work rationalisation, seeking more productive machinery, and reducing the size and skills of the work force, is less and less adequate; corporate survival is now dependent on the location of production at sites where labour power is cheap, plentiful, well-disciplined and acquiescent. Rationalisation at home and productive relocation abroad are twin strategies with the same objective, and each strategy can support the other, in that location abroad, or the threat of it, can have consequences for the attitudes and commitment of the original work force.

Numerous writers (most notably Braverman) have noted how the principles of Taylorism – deskilling, fragmentation, task specification, etc. – reflect and help to achieve the objectives of capitalism through cheapening labour, making it more productive, more transferable and less central to the decision-making side of the production process. But Frobel *et al.* make a further point: these principles are now increasingly applied by corporate management on an international, no longer a merely national, basis. Calculations about investment, work design, technologies, are now made on a global basis: '...the present-day conditions for the world-wide valorisation of capital mean that capital must completely recalculate the allocation of the elements of the manufacturing process to the most advantageous combination of 'factors of production' as regards the cost of the final product, *on a global basis* – taking into account the enormous reserve army of less skilled workers which has recently come into existence. In many instances, the end result of this calculaton...will be the relocation of industrial production (and subassembly) to new sites, chiefly in the developing countries with their practically inexhaustible reservoir of unskilled and extremely cheap labour-power.' (Frobel *et al.* 1980, p. 133)

There can be no doubt that in the developing countries, labour is cheap, hardworking and congenial. Listen to an investment brochure from Malaysia: 'Oriental women are famous throughout the world for their dexterity. With their small hands, they work fast and pay great attention to detail. Who could be better qualified by nature and tradition to raise the efficiency of an assembly line?...Wage rates in Malaysia are among the lowest in the region, and women-workers can be employed for about U.S. $1.50 a day.' (quoted by Lipietz, 1982, p. 42.) Workers in many third world societies are 'superexploited' – that is, they are not even paid enough to sustain them and their families, but are subsidised by the labour of other members of their families (Frank, 1981, pp. 157-87). Super-exploitation of third world workers has a number of implications. They work more hours than their counterparts in the West; Frobel *et al.* calculate that they receive between 10% and 20% of wages in the traditional industrial societies; usually they can be hired and fired at will (Frobel *et al.,* 1980, pp. 34-5). Often, the host society can offer 'attractive' anti-union legislation; internal work control can be supported by external policing, unionists can be harassed; 'trouble-makers' persecuted; space and safety provisions are frequently much less than can be expected in the West. A comparison of wage levels, hours of work, safety provisions, fringe benefits etc. – between work and working conditions in the underdeveloped countries and in the traditional industrial societies – shows that 'Working conditions...compel the labour-force in free production zones and world market factories in the underdeveloped countries...to achieve levels of productivity and intensity of labour which correspond to the most advanced current levels in the world, and to...tolerate wage levels which are not much higher than those which prevailed in Manchester capitalism's heyday.' (Frobel *et al.,* 1980, p. 36.)

Thus a characteristic feature of corporate decision-making and corporate strategy in late capitalism is the 'rationalisation' of labour and work at home and the transfer of industry to areas abroad where labour is cheaper and can be 'super-exploited', with consequences for wage rates, accidents, working conditions, and most significantly, profits. What implications does this transfer of investments have for the quality of work? Are there any relations between capital's efforts to increase control over labour at home, and the transfer of investments overseas? We shall now turn to a consideration of these questions. Three points must be made,

First, the preceding section makes it clear that the modern firm is now international in its organisation, and that corporate decisions about what, how and where to produce and to market, take place on the basis of global calculations of costs, benefits and profits. This development means that it is no longer feasible to conduct a complete analysis, or explanation of a particular organisation, or indeed of employing organisations within any particular economy, without consideration of the location of that corporation, and that economy, within a global division of labour. As we shall see, and as Frobel *et al.*, Frank, and Mandel describe, it is not possible to restrict an analysis of a Texas Instruments factory in Taiwan, or a National factory in Malaysia, a textile mill in any Free Production Zone anywhere in Asia, Africa or Latin America, simply to local conditions, markets, and economies. Increasingly it is true that what occurs within and to a particular enterprise, or indeed to a particular economy or industry, can only be understood in terms of the global division of labour within which it is situated.

Secondly, and more specifically, any analysis of working conditions within factories in third world countries must recognise that these conditions – this level of 'super-exploitation' – is not merely an accident of geography, an unfortunate and passing 'stage' in development, or an outcome of some purely local combination of culture, history and national character, nor an outcome of some national moral deficiency – the lack of 'drive' so over-developed elsewhere. The working conditions under which so many third world workers suffer are a systematic outcome of a global division of labour whereby the continuing impoverishment of the third world – or at least of most societies within this category – is often encouraged and reproduced by the investment and production policies of multinational corporations. Frobel *et al.* report, for example, that on the basis of their investigation of the local benefits of world industrialisation and the emergence of numerous Free Production Zones, 'Whereas...the economic yields for the countries concerned are in most cases slight and in some cases even negative, corporate profits are massive. As a result of the industrial enclave character of world market oriented industry, corporate profits do not even indirectly increase the local national income, for example through reinvestment, and conversely negative developments in the local domestic economies have hardly any impact on the rate of corporate profitability.' (Frobel *et al.* 1980, p. 378.)

For any consideration of the inequalities of working life, this conclusion is very serious indeed. It means that we cannot, under the auspices of such an enquiry, restrict our attention to the (relatively) privileged West.

Furthermore, as numerous writers have recently noted, the 'survival' in various guises, of forms of labour and of labour/capitalist relationship which ostensibly seem characteristic of pre-capitalist economic forms, is a direct and systematic outcome of the global division of labour. The 'super-exploitation' described by Frank, Frobel *et al.*, and Mandel involves three key elements: increase in the intensity of work; extension of the working day, and payment of labour below its value (Osorio, quoted in Frank, 1981, p. 161). Frequently super-exploitation is accompanied by oppressive, coercive control of labour itself. As Corrigan has argued, the expansion of capitalism means the expansion of unfree labour: 'Unfree labour is not a feudal relic, but part of the essential relations of capitalism.' (Corrigan, 1977, p. 438.) Such unfree labour takes a variety of shapes: historically, workers having the status of indentured servants; forms of slavery or forced migration; migration as coercive circulation; or the employment of migrant workers or guestworkers. The point about such workers is their exposure and vulnerability to some degree of legalised coercion in their work relationships. Unlike the classic labourer who is 'free' (legally) to terminate his or her employment, the unfree labourer finds such freedom circumscribed by law, indenture, immigration policy, and similar restrictions.

The expansion of capitalism into new areas does not necessarily involve traditional forms of coercive control. For example, the willingness of some companies to finance the setting up of factories in mainland China indicates a corresponding willingness to trade ownership and direct control for other benefits. Processing contracts, whereby the Chinese agree to supply a certain quantity of product for, say, five years in return for capital equipment and working capital, provides a guaranteed source of supply to the foreign firm and offloads all problems of labour control and labour effort onto a socialist state (Lockett and Littler, 1984).

Thirdly, if working conditions in Third World countries are seen as part of a global division of labour, then by the same token, working conditions in the West are related directly to conditions prevailing elsewhere. This relationship has a number of aspects. We have remarked that rationalisation at home and investment abroad are part of the same process: the search for profits under competition. Also, investment abroad affects workers and working conditions at home both directly, in that it may mean the export of jobs, and more indirectly in that the threat to invest overseas can and frequently has been used – for example by Fords – to discipline workers, win concessions and strengthen management's hand during negotiations. Workers in the traditional industrial countries will thus be exposed to labour intensification and to unemployment, and their resistance undermined by the threat of further foreign investment. Frobel *et al.* calculate, for example, that a conservative estimate of foreign employment by German productive industry is 1.5-1.6 million workers in 1975, and report that 'Falling or stagnating employment in Federal Germany, and rising employment abroad have characterised developments in many companies for a number of years, especially the large combines.' (Frobel *et al.*, 1980, pp. 285-6.) Unemployment, redundancies, short-time working, declining real incomes at home; abroad, unemployment, underemployment, 'super-exploitation', and deskilled, simplified tasks – the multinational corporation with its international profit calculations can be responsible for all these effects.

Multinationals provide a framework and a calculus for determining comparative labour productivities. For example, the British Chloride company, which started the 1970s as a predominantly home-based organisation, embarked on a major programme of acquisitions abroad between 1972 and 1975. This involved the takeover of about ten companies in Europe, five in North America and others in Australia and South Africa. Within the space of a few years the Chloride group was a multinational with a reorganised management structure. One of the most obvious results of this multinational development was the management's ability to measure the performance of British workers against those in its overseas subsidiaries. In 1977 this led to the introduction of new intensified work practices and effort norms, which in turn drove the normally peaceable workforce into a two month strike and occupation of the factories (*The Financial Times*, 22 July 1977). This availability of international comparisons leads to a world-wide commodification of labour.

The role of the state

The third major feature of capital's response to increasing competitive pressure, during late capitalism, is an attack on organised labour. We have noted that in a sense the first two strategies, rationalisation and foreign investment, also carry implications for the control of labour both directly through increased rationalisation and surveillance, and indirectly through the capacity to locate production in areas with 'good' industrial relations records. However, alongside these initiatives, the period of late capitalism also demonstrates an increase in state attacks on labour and on labour unions, both direct and indirect. It is to these state initiatives that we now turn.

In general we find that this period is also, and relatedly, one of greatly increased state intervention. Mandel argues that the shortening of the turnover time of fixed capital, the acceleration of technological innovation, and the increase in the cost of major projects, produces '...an inherent trend under late capitalism for the state to incorporate an ever greater number of productive and reproductive sectors into the "general conditions of production" which it finances.' (Mandel, 1978, p. 484.) State economic interventions have taken a number of forms: collective provision (of such things as welfare, housing, health services,) demand management to achieve a 'satisfactory' level of unemployment, demand, inflation, etc., and central planning, to achieve co-ordination, develop investment and reduce market anarchy.

However, such increased state intervention is not necessarily the neutral, merely technical operation it is often presented as. As we have noted, a critical feature of modern capitalism and the economic crises it is experiencing is the struggle between labour and capital, and its potential impact on levels of profitability. Under these conditions, capital attempts to tighten control over the production process and over production costs (including, crucially, labour costs).

The state usually plays a major part in relations between capital and labour, by seeking both to limit the power of labour in struggles and negotiations and to influence the outcomes of these. Such interventions, of whatever nature, are all occasioned by the declining rate of profit, and by the fact that this is recognised to be partly due to the increased strength of organised labour. State interventions therefore are aimed directly at reducing this strength, and at persuading workers to accept less money for more work.

These interventions take a number of forms: ideological attacks; attacks on organised, that is unionised, labour, direct efforts to reduce wages, and attacks on welfare provisions. These elements are frequently closely connected, such as to constitute strands of a recognisable political platform, increasingly adoped by conservative and other parties under the slogans of 'less government'. Ironically, many state efforts to reduce the power of organised labour are justified by reference to the advantages of reduced government intervention in economic life.

Ideologically, the new conservatism argues the neutrality of the economy, and the powerlessness of governments in the face of overwhelming economic forces. Clearly, to argue that direct economic Keynesian interventions are impossible would, in the light of post 1930s government economic policies, be ludicrous. What is argued instead is that such Keynesian interventions actually compound the problem − inflation/unemployment − *in the long run*. The economy is defined in moralistic terms. Its pathologies are occasioned by overindulgence, undeserved extravagance on a societal level. The solution is to strip away the paraphernalia of government intervention and support, the 'artificial' creation of demand, for these only increase the tendency to inflation. The causes are defined in terms highly analogous to those applicable to individual immorality − greed, over-indulgence, extravagance. The problem itself is never in doubt: it is inflation, the consequence of licence.

This view has a number of key elements: that the economy is essentially analogous to an individual's earning and consumption patterns, writ large; that individual extravagance is responsible for large scale economic problems; that the major problem, the number one issue, is inflation; that this can only be conquered by permitting the re-emergence and ascendancy of basic economic forces too long masked by the interventions of governments seeking to buy short term solutions; that an untrammeled economy, wherein the forces of supply and demand are allowed unrestricted movement, and where individuals' basic entrepreneurial instincts are permitted free rein, is the only means of ensuring ultimate, long term, economic 'health'.

These ideas have very definite implications. First, they seek to depoliticise

the responsibility of government for economic matters. Such matters—
levels of unemployment, recession, bankruptcies, inflation, interest rates, etc.
are defined as (a) the consequence of earlier governments' attempts to buy
their way out of trouble by stimulating demand artificially; (b) the
consequence of individuals' greed, laziness, etc. They are presented then as
not being related to current government philosophies, or action. Such
action seeks simply to re-establish a state of affairs wherein these problems
will ultimately disappear.

Secondly, they present the problems themselves as unfortunate
consequences of individuals', and earlier governments', misguided courses
of action. The government is not responsible and is unable, even if willing,
to intervene productively without actually exacerbating matters. Thirdly,
these ideas define the major problem as being inflation — as symptom of our
times, a consequence of our unrealistic expectations, our unwillingness to
pay our way in the world, our unwillingness to earn the luxuries we aspire
to.

These ideological efforts have a second major strand. This concerns the
nature and function of unions, and relations between labour and capital.
Unions are defined as having exceeded their proper role, as having grown
too strong (and thus being largely responsible for inflation by enabling
workers to gain benefits greater than those they 'deserve' by their efforts).
Unions are seen in the same light as Keynesian economic policies—as
interfering with the necessary re-establishment of the basic economic
forces—supply and demand—through the imposition of over-manning, the
closed shop, etc. Furthermore, on many occasions, relations between labour
and capital, when these become explicitly relations of conflict, are not
defined in terms of industrial relations, class conflict, negotiations over
levels of pay, but are regarded as threats to law and order, or relatedly, as
issues of freedom. As such they often become open to the intervention of the
police to ensure the maintenance of law and order, and the courts, to
protect individuals' (usually employers') 'rights'. These definitions have
importance in reducing the strength of labour's capacity to resist and
organise successfully, quite apart from their direct impact on each particular
struggle. For such ideas serve to weaken support for unions by holding them
responsible for large-scale economic ills; and seek to make illegitimate the
issues and resources and strategies typically employed in industrial disputes.

The ideological elements described above are accompanied by more
concrete developments in law which seek to reduce such hard-won
concessions as have been won by unions, and to make unions more
vulnerable to employers' tactics in industrial disputes, and to governmental
control. Once again the law is used to buttress employers' strength in
industrial conflicts and negotiations and to attack directly any union tactic
which might have proved to be of particular use, such as secondary
picketing.

Attempts to lower the price of labour take two classic forms, used as functional alternatives: direct intervention by government in levels of wage increases through formal wage control or varieties of 'social contract'; and indirect, through allowing an increase in unemployment to take place.

The point of wage control, whatever form these efforts may take, is quite clear, and has been frequently reiterated by government spokesmen: it is to push down real wages below the levels of inflation — in short, to reduce the price of labour and to lower real incomes. However, the experience of successive governments throughout the seventies demonstrated the two major weaknesses of all forms of wage freeze or wage control, regardless of how they were presented to workers and voters: firstly, wage control does not work over long periods, but merely delays workers' demands; and secondly, it tends to encourage politicised conflict between employees and unions on the one side and the government of the day on the other. The explicit intervention of governments in relations between labour and capital, no matter how this may be defined by government spokesmen as necessary for the 'national' good, and as an attack on 'extremist' unionists, nevertheless inevitably forces direct confrontation with labour, and government itself may be the loser (as in the 1974 general election, called on the platform — 'Who runs the country?'). The record of the seventies also shows however that without some form of wage control the relative strength of labour in relation to capital is increased and unionised labour is consequently able to achieve considerable improvements in wages thus, ultimately, occasioning a reduction in capital's profitability. The solution to this dilemma — that wage control is necessary for capital but too dangerous and ineffective to apply — lies in the functional alternative to wage control: unemployment.

In arguing that unemployment represents a strategy, rather than an unfortunate and unavoidable development outside the control of any government, it is necessary to show that unemployment is at least in part attributable to government policies on wages and government spending, and that increasing levels of 'natural' unemployment play a major part in reducing workers' bargaining strength and, hence, their wage claims. Concerning the origins of mass unemployment, it is important to note, as Glyn and Sutcliffe point out, that this increase is not simply the consequence of technological development, with jobs being automated. Automation only means mass unemployment when market stagnation leads to old plant (and workers) being scrapped to make way for new, which would not occur if markets were expanding. As these authors remark: 'The fundamental cause of the massive rise in unemployment under Labour was a major slowdown in the rate at which markets, and hence production, grew. Government spending and workers' consumption stagnated because of conscious government policies.' (Glyn and Harrison, 1980, pp. 127-8.) It is, however, with the policies of the Thatcher government that the use of unemployment and other anti-labour policies achieves its fullest expression.

Thatcherism as a political philosophy contains a number of discrete elements, the most important of which are monetarist economic policy, and reduced public spending and state support for nationalised industry. The justification of these policies is that with credit difficult to find, and more expensive, inefficient firms go out of business; production is concentrated in efficient sectors and efficient firms; management is forced to rationalise organisation and production. At the same time, workers' confidence and aspirations are reduced: 'People are understandably reluctant to take a tough stand on job conditions if bankruptcy seems possible and the chances of finding another job are low.' (Glyn and Harrison, 1980, p. 139.) At the same time the strength of unions is undermined, in practical terms, by high unemployment among union members, which irrespective of members' willingness, reduces unions' income and their capacity to finance industrial action.

There can be no doubt that government ministers are and were well aware of the role of unemployment in the struggles between labour and capital, and sought deliberately to use this strategy to 'cool off' expectations and to reduce bargaining strength. Gunder Frank points to 'Essentially the same austerity policy of deliberate recession, masquerading behind a fig leaf of "fighting inflation"' (Frank, 1980, p. 113). He goes on to make the central point, revealing the ideological and practical aspects of monetarist policy—that it reduces worker strength, while at the same time disguising its origins and implications: 'Capital's real intention is not to combat inflation, which is created by monopoly capital and helps all capital reduce real wages. The real point is to increase profits by reducing real wages through various means, including inflation and unemployment. However, to the extent that it is still impolitic to admit to wanting to increase unemployment, it sounds better to say that inflation is public enemy number one.' (Frank, 1980, p. 124.) As he also remarks, a major element in the ideological side of this offensive is to decrease public concern about unemployment: by re-defining 'natural', therefore unavoidable, rates of unemployment, asserting that it was an international problem, not merely a British one; by asserting its links with (neutral and unavoidable) technological developments—the notorious 'chip' in particular; and by linking unemployment with militant industrial action and with 'irresponsible' wage demands. These ideas could be given considerable edge when allied with attacks on 'scroungers'. In this way the general problem of unemployment, and each individual case, could be defined as the consequences of economic forces unleashed through collective and individual greed and immorality.

Conclusions

This chapter has attempted to describe the basic dynamics of contemporary capitalism as these have impact on corporate strategy, and the development of work forms and modes of organisation. The starting point for the analysis was the centrality of profit for the capitalist enterprise, and the inevitable significance this has for relations between labour and capital. The fact of profit as the mainspring of capitalism places capital and labour in definitionally conflictful relations though there may be no actual conflict taking place between employers and workers. The chapter considered recent trends in levels of overall profitability, and assessed the impact of the recent crisis in profitability on corporate strategy. It was stressed that corporate efforts to increase profitability under crisis conditions take at least two major forms: labour intensification, technological innovation and the rationalisation of work design and procedures; and the international movement of capital. Both occur within the context of increased state interventions in management/worker relations.

Throughout, it has been stressed that efforts to improve profits are at the same time efforts to improve control, either through increased specification of effort (or through re-locating production in areas where such specification can be more easily achieved) or through influencing worker attitudes and commitment. Any attempt by capital to solve its problems of profitability, and particularly the two forms of solution most frequently adopted by the large, multinational corporations which increasingly dominate the economies of the advanced industrial societies, inevitably involves the basic relation between capital and labour, and represents an attempt by capital to re-order the relative strengths and advantages of this relationship in its favour. Such efforts are considerably assisted by the increasing intervention of the state in this relationship. However, as we have suggested, they raise certain recurring contradictions, the main one being the tension between the two essential but to some degree mutually incompatible dimensions of control, which will be treated in the next chapter.

4 · Capitalism and the Control of Work

Chapter 3 argued that in general under capitalism the employers' requirements to achieve and realise profit had consequences for the structuring of work in ways which were both productive of profit and which ensured the continuance of the existing economic order. That chapter also argued, however, that under conditions of economic crisis, the pressure on employers to arrange production so as to eliminate 'wastage' and maximise 'efficiency' — both defined in terms of increasing the relative advantage of capital in the capital/labour relationship — would be exacerbated. It was noted that under these conditions, firms would seek to improve their efficiency by recourse to internal and external measures; and indeed, that these developments were likely to be buttressed by the activities (or the lack of activity) of the State.

But the chapter also made a more basic point, one which will reverberate throughout the remainder of this book and will attract particular attention in this chapter. The point concerns the *nature* of work control under capital — a characteristic which has up to now been largely undeveloped. What are the characteristics of work control under capitalism? That issue constitutes the theme of this chapter.

Co-ordination and control

The need for co-ordination in modern industrial organisations is partly a consequence of the increasing division of labour. Under handicraft production a worker who fashions a complete product does not need to co-ordinate his labour with other workers, except in a minimal way. Work patterns and work pace can be flexible and relatively self-determined. However, specialisation and fragmentation of work intensify the problems of co-ordination: 'Specialisation has a centrifugal influence on organisation; it fractures the central unity of the work process.' (Dubin, 1958, p. 48.) The increasing specialisation and fragmentation of work has been, of course, tied in with the development of the modern factory system.

The modern factory represents a concentration of capital and labour plus the application of power. However, many accounts of the industrial revolution give a misleading picture of the nature and evolution of the modern factory. A more accurate typology of factory development is the one suggested by Chapman, which is as follows.

Type 1: Centralised workshops
This describes single-process, centralised workshops, such as the mediaeval fulling mill. In the seventeenth and eighteenth centuries there emerged workshops for dyeing, stocking frames, tape looms etc., all of which represented a concentration of capital. Chapman points out that one cannot grasp the essence of these workshops in terms of the use and application of power. Some workshops used power machinery, and some (e.g. tape looms, stocking frames) did not. Nor did the use of powered machinery necessarily imply a greater fixed capital investment than with the use of manually-operated machines: the simple mills of the period rarely generated more than ten-horse-power and seldom represented an investment of more than £100 to £200, which was a sum often surpassed in other manual workshops (Chapman, 1974, p. 471).

Type 2: Proto-factories
This refers to workshops where there is a centralisation of several production processes, usually for reasons of enhanced employer control, and where an extensive sub-division of labour has not yet occurred. In such workshops 'sometimes mechanical power was used, and sometimes manual, and quite often a combination of both.' (ibid., p. 471.) Chapman calls this type of production unit a 'proto-factory'. The proto-factory was widespread in several industries before 1775, and the fully evolved factory (see Type 3 below) made its appearance only slowly.

Type 3: Mass production factories
This is the fully-developed factory system. Chapman regards the essential characteristic of this type of production system as being that it entailed an extensive division of labour, tied to a system of flow production rather than batch production methods: 'flow production means that machines and equipment have been arranged in line sequence to process goods continuously through a sequence of specialised operations.' (ibid., p. 470.) In addition, the machine/product relation has consequences for the man/product relation: the inter-linked semi-automatic machinery was tended by semi-skilled or unskilled workers with a nucleus of skilled workers to maintain the machinery and direct the plant. The utilisation of mechanical power is *not* the feature which distinguishes the fully-evolved factory from earlier production systems. Power is essential to the modern factory because the continuous synchronisation of a sequence of highly-specialised machines could not be achieved by other means: thus it is a necessary characteristic, not a sufficient one. The spread of the modern factory system was so slow that it can be identified in only one non-textile industry before 1815.

Chapman's work suggests a typology of the modes of organising the labour process which is set out in Table 1.

Table 1 *Modes of organising the labour process*

Mode of organisation of the labour process	Concentration of capital	Concentration of labour	Single process/ multi-process	Flow production
Small workshop production	Dispersed	Dispersed	Multi-process	Absent
Domestic system	Concentrated in hands of merchants or factors	Dispersed	Mixed, tending towards single process	Absent
Single process, centralised workshops – Type 1	Relatively concentrated	Concentrated	Single-process	Absent
Proto-factory – Type 2	Relatively concentrated	Concentrated	Multi-process	Absent
Modern mass production factory – Type 3	Highly concentrated	Concentrated	Multi-process, tending towards process specialisation	Present

The definition of modern production systems in Table 1 implies that the logic of industrialism was slow to work itself out. Thus Chapman emphasises that 'even in the cotton industry it was to take another half century before the implications of Arkwright's basic idea were fully worked out.' (ibid., p. 473.) Moreover, the pattern of development in cotton textiles was no more than the harbinger of future developments, rather than the typical form adopted by other industries. Many industries, like the Birmingham and Sheffield trades, retained a structure of small workshops and enterprises, which involved personal and diffuse relations of subordination (see Littler, 1982, Chapter 6). As Hannah argues, 'It was not until the later era of large machine tools, engineering standardisation and the assembly line that they were to gain access to internal economies of scale comparable to (and indeed greater than) those in the cotton industry.' (Hannah, 1976, p. 10.) What this implies is that there continued to be a dispersal of labour and of industrial capital across many small intensely competitive firms: it is not until the 1880-1914 period that we first see the development of the fully-evolved factory system in most industries.

There is one control feature of the increasing division of labour and the development of the labour process through the nineteenth and early twentieth centuries which has been theoretically examined by Claus Offe. The basic distinction used by Offe is that between 'task-continuous status organisation' and 'task-discontinuous status organisation'. In the former type, 'the relation between the positions is such that there is a wide area of technical rules to which equal obedience is required from all occupants of the positions.' Moreover, a superordinate position differs from a subordinate position 'merely in that it is defined in terms of greater mastery of the rules and greater ability, knowledge and experience in production.' (Offe, 1976, p. 25.) Offe suggests that the small craft workshop, with a hierarchy of apprentice, journeyman and master, typifies the task-continuous form of organisation. Contrasted with the above is the task-discontinuous form, which involves a set of incongruent superior/subordinate skills and knowledge, such that superiors in the hierarchy of authority no longer have a claim to greater competence at the technical methods of work. Thus, there is no longer a simple hierarchy, instead there is a separation of hierarchical and functional organisation (ibid., pp. 25-27). Given this distinction, the argument is that with the development of the labour process there has been a widespread shift from task-continuous to task-discontinuous forms of work organisation.

Offe's argument is partly right and partly wrong. Firstly, his historical schema is over-simplified and somewhat misleading. There have always been elements of incongruency of superior/subordinate skills and task-knowledge. By focusing on the small, craft workshop Offe ignores the work situation of the majority, in which there frequently was a sharp divide between the gentleman-farmer, or the Chinese Confucian scholar, and the peasant in the fields. Equally, the argument ignores the period of merchant capitalism when the factors and merchants were frequently in a position of technical ignorance and often relied on subcontracting, both internal and external, and the domestic system in order to get the work out. On the other side of the coin, it is not always the case that the development of modern industrial organisation has entailed a decrease in the congruency of superior/subordinate skills. Japanese industrial organisations with an hierarchy of, say, drill operators, promoted foremen/gang-leaders, and engineering-trained department managers represents the opposite type of hierarchy. Thus the patterns of change have been more complex than those assumed by Offe. Nevertheless, despite these qualifications, the broad trend which Offe is seeking to mark out theoretically, from task-continuous to task-discontinuous organisation, is probably correct.

The basic control implication of the reduced congruency of skills is that workers' task performance becomes less 'observable' — supervisors cannot easily tell whether an operator is doing a good job or working at a proper speed. This employer problem has led to two alternatives: the development of systematic monitoring systems, or increased potential work autonomy resulting in the need for enhanced ideological control. Offe opts for the latter path of development, but this response has not been the typical one, as we will argue in Chapter 5.

Apart from the unforeseen consequences of the elaboration of task-discontinuous work organisation, the synchronisation of fragmented tasks is fundamental to the industrial work process. This synchronisation becomes part of a new time order very different from the natural time order of earlier agrarian societies. Thus, E. P. Thompson suggests that traditional attitudes to work involved a disregard for clock time, and that the 'day's tasks...seem to disclose themselves, by the logic of need, before the crofter's eyes.' He calls this attitude 'task-orientation'. It involves three characteristics: —

> First, there is a sense in which it is more humanly comprehensible than timed labour. The peasant or labourer appears to attend upon what is an observed necessity. Second, a community in which task-orientation is common appears to show least demarcation between 'work' and 'life'. Social intercourse and labour are intermingled. ...Third, to men accustomed to labour timed by the clock, this attitude to labour appears to be wasteful and lacking in urgency.
>
> (E. P. Thompson, 1967, p. 59.)

Task orientation is based on the independent peasant or craftsman, but as soon as wage labour occurs there is a marked shift to a new sense of time. Time becomes money — the employer's money. As Thompson puts it, 'Those who are employed experience a distinction between their employer's time and their "own" time. And the employer must use the time of his labour, and see it is not wasted: not the task but the value of time when reduced to money is dominant. Time is now currency: it is not passed but spent.' (ibid., p. 60.)

The early industrialists, then, were concerned with breaking down the popular work culture of irregular, varied work patterns with alternative bouts of intense labour and idleness, and the continued celebration of 'St. Monday.' Instead there was an effort to form new labour habits and inculcate a new time discipline. Thus the opposite of a task-orientation is a time orientation. The latter orientation in its extreme form is reflected in the following quotation:

> Time:
> Measure your time, control it!
> Do everything on time! exactly on the minute!
> Save time, make time count, work fast!
> Divide your time correctly, time for work
>   and time for leisure!
> Utilize your leisure so as to work better
>   afterwards!

This was part of a pamphlet issued by the 'Time League' in Russia in 1923. The Time League was concerned with the massive shift of the Russian people from a task orientation to a time orientation, as a crash social programme (Bendix, 1974, p. 208).

Thompson's basic distinction between a task orientation, with its sense of inevitable tasks and natural rhythms, and a time orientation, with its pressing need to co-ordinate activities with the abstract passage of time, is theoretically useful, but time-orientation is not an 'all or nothing' process. Time discipline has to be continually reproduced in each generation, and the entire control problem was intensified with the introduction of the stop-watch and the institutionalisation of Taylorism (see Chapter 5).

However, what is important and what can be drawn out of Thompson's work, is that the creation of a new time order is an essential aspect of the industrial control problem – a problem which intensified during the 1880-1914 period as the first stages of assembly-line production made their appearance. Keeping pace with machine cycles and conveyor speeds became the daily struggle for thousands of workers.

So far, we have argued that the increasing division of labour associated with the development and spread of the modern factory system entailed severe problems of co-ordination and labour control. Two aspects of this process – the relative increase in task-discontinuous organisation and the increasing need to develop a new time-orientation – intensified these control problems. The problems of factory discipline and co-ordination were inserted into the capital/wage labour relationship. Work is not just a technical relation, but a power relation. As such it is structured by the power inequalities of the wider society. The next section examines the capital/labour relationship in the work context.

The capital/labour relation

When a worker sells his or her labour to an employer in exchange for wages, the exchange is inherently 'incomplete', for what is being sold is not a precisely specified number and quality and type of work operation, but a preparedness to conform to the employer's demands within the bounds of capacity, skill, strength, knowledge, dexterity, etc. In other words the worker exchanges a potential, a preparedness which the employer directs and organises. Now this simple and obvious feature of any and all employment exchanges renders the employer dependent – to a greater or lesser degree – on the motivation, attitudes, work orientation, of the employee. For without some (highly variable) degree of acquiescence, of willingness to co-operate, the employer finds the employee's potential is not being realised in the intensities and forms which he – the employer – desires.

In other words, the subjectivity of the employee is – and must be – an inevitable ingredient in the organisation of work, the achievement of production at work, in relations between managers and workers, capital and labour. As such it must be a central element in control relationships.

The key concept delineating the essential non-exchange nature of the capitalist economy is the labour/labour-power distinction. The commodity which the worker sells is not a fixed amount of labour embodied in a complete product but 'labour power', i.e. the capacity to work. Thus the commodity which is exchanged in the marketplace (labour power) is not the same entity which enters into the production process (labour). There is a central indeterminacy of labour potential, an indefiniteness that must be resolved in other ways. Edwards stresses this point: 'Labour power can be bought, but between the purchase of labour power and the real appropriation of useful labour comes a wedge: the will, motivation and consciousness of the worker drastically affects the work force's productivity'. (Edwards, 1974, p. 111.) To translate legal ownership into real possession the employer must erect structures of control over labour.

Some forms of employer control are necessary because conflict is structured into the labour process. The material basis of that conflict lies in the fact that there can be no long-term agreement over wage/effort exchanges – the process of production in the context of capitalist competition involves continuous conflict over the terms and the ways in which employers extract effort from workers. For example one observer, who worked on the assembly line at Toyota's car plant in Japan, records that:

> The working system has changed three times in six months. Until August, there was a single daytime shift. From September to December there were two shifts, a day shift and an evening shift immediately following it. Now there is a day-night shift system that allows the company to get the workers to work lots of overtime on both shifts. And the management never consulted the workers in any way before making these changes. They increased production without increasing the number of workers simply by requiring more overtime work.
>
> (Satoshi Kamata, 1982, p. 118.)

However, the emphasis on the conflictual nature of the labour process has been criticised by some recent writers, notably Burawoy (1979) and Cressey & MacInnes (1980). The argument here is that as all work relations involve elements of co-operation, it is a curiously one-sided approach to stress conflict. Burawoy asserts that it is necessary 'to dispense with metaphysical assumptions about underlying conflict or harmony' (ibid., p. 12), and goes on to argue that the labour process must be understood not only in terms of conflict and resistance but also in terms of the generation of consent (ibid., p. 30). Clearly a 'reverse problematic' which starts with consent challenges the notion that the development of the capitalist production process inevitably results in class consciousness (Thompson, 1983, p. 157).

This form of argument has been elaborated by writers such as the Ehrenreichs (1976), who stress that modern work systems *both* collectivise and atomise the labour force. The atomising effects of modern work organisation arise from the serial organisation of production; the fact that some hierarchical and isolating effects are built into the technology itself, and from conscious management strategies to isolate and fragment workers socially. Such factors lead to a dispersion of any collective consciousness and to the 'flight from work' described by Göran Palm (1977); in other words to mass privatisation. But what has been added by Burawoy is the notion that the generation of consent is intrinsic to the labour process itself.

The argument has been advanced by two recent writers, Cressey & MacInnes (1980), who suggest a contradictory relationship between capital and labour, rather than a uni-dimensional view of conflict-generation. According to them, capitalists are faced with the problems of continually transforming the forces of production. This, in turn, entails stimulating motivation and harnessing labour's creative and productive powers. Thus capitalists must to some degree seek a co-operative relationship with labour. They cannot just exploit those capacities which can be brought into play by bribery and coercion. Similarly, side-by-side with labour's resistance to subordination lies the fact that workers have an interest in the maintenance of the capital/labour relation and the viability of the units of capital which employ them. In summary: 'The two-fold nature of the relationship of capital to labour in the workplace implies *directly contradictory* strategies for both labour and capital which in turn represent the working out of the contradictions between the forces and relations of production at the level of the workplace itself.' (Cressey & MacInnes, 1980, p.14.)

In other words, workers are simultaneously involved in two different relationships – a wage/effort relationship entailing conflict and control and an employment relationship entailing (potential) unity of interests with competitors. Equally, employers face a contradiction in that maximising control minimises initiative and reliability and discredits the employment relationship.

Even Frederick Taylor recognised that no system of management could entirely dispense with the initiative ('hard-work, good-will and ingenuity') of the workers, though Taylor showed a peculiar naivety about people, in that he hoped to achieve increased organisational commitment whilst restricting worker discretion to a minimum *(Principles,* pp. 34-7).

If the contradictory nature of the capital/labour relationship is accepted, then this changes the character of the control relation. Control must be seen in relation to conflict *and* in relation to the potential terrain of compromise and compliance. What is at issue here is precisely what sort of work control is necessary under capitalism. According to Braverman, echoing Taylor, work control under capitalism requires the ever more pervasive, oppressive and detailed prescription of levels and direction of work performance. Control, essentially, requires rules, although in most cases these rules are so embedded in machinery or work flow as to be aspects of technology. But are rules enough? Within other traditions of sociological interest in work organisations, or relations at the workplace, it is a truism that no rule, or body of rules, is ever precise enough entirely and accurately to constrain and guide behaviour. A considerable and important body of work within industrial and organisational sociology testifies to what any manager knows well enough: rules are not sufficient. First, rules themselves tend to be used when other forms of control have broken down, and they can then be used not only to guide performance but to establish minima (Gouldner, 1963). Secondly, all rules rely on some element of judgement. It is for this reason that 'working to rule' is, in the real world, if not in recent sociology of the labour process, a form of industrial resistance.

Numerous authors have pointed to the 'incompleteness' of rules as guides to action: the inevitable persistence of some areas of discretion and uncertainty (see, for example, Crozier, 1964, Blau, 1963, Gouldner 1954; many of these works are summarised in Salaman, 1979). Thirdly, given the peculiar quality of labour power as a 'factor of production', it is clear that even the most specific ˙ and all-embracing regime of work-based prescriptions cannot but rely on the preparedness of the worker to expend his or her effort. For work rules to play any part in directing effort the workers must first expend effort. This 'motivational' or attitudinal side is entirely lacking in many recent analyses.

To assert the importance of workers' attitudes is not to suggest the liberalisation of management, or any reduction of management concern with the achievement of surplus value. It is simply to argue that the achievement of surplus depends upon management efforts to obtain certain conditions in the work-place – most importantly, to achieve some sort, and some level of consent.

To argue, as we do, that all forms of collective labour within capitalism depend on both the development of some level of consent and some degree of specification of levels, direction and quantities of performance is not the same as the more conventional argument that capitalism entails a greater variety of forms of control than the one – scientific management – envisaged by Braverman. According to this argument capitalism offers a variety of strategies of control.

We argue however that *all* forms of control contain, in different degree, two dimensions of control: the specification of levels of performance (and this may vary from highly specified, to highly autonomous) and some effort to develop some level of consent, or acceptance of the legitimacy of the employment relationship. Both these dimensions are necessary for any work relationship. The utility of the specification of levels of performance depends absolutely on some minimal level of compliance.

To argue this is not to deny the reality and frequency of worker resistance, sabotage, withdrawal, etc. Nor is it to assert the satisfaction of most workers with their work. But it is to take seriously, as requiring explanation, *de facto* acquiescence in the basic elements of the employment relationship. Of course employees are not as they sometimes appear in Braverman's analysis. But equally they are not as resistant to work control and subordination and inequalities of work as some writers have insisted. We may choose to regard all manifestations of discontent and withdrawal as, ultimately, class based and evidence of some level of class consciousness. But it remains true, as Burawoy and many other observers of modern work organisations have noted, that the phenomenon that needs to be explained is not the occasional outburst of resistance, the levels of absenteeism, the restriction of output, but the fact that employees do not resist more, that they are prepared to commit their energy to a degree which is acceptable to employers. To make this simple and obvious point is not to deny that, ultimately, relations between buyers and sellers of labour are antagonistic. But it is to assert the importance in practice of discovering the conditions under which these potentials are realised. To remain at the level of abstract assertion of class antagonisms is misleading in an analysis of work relations, because, as Burawoy notes, the interests that organise the daily life of workers are not given irrevocably; they cannot be imputed; they are produced and reproduced in particular ways (Burawoy, 1978, p. 257).

Remaining at the level of abstract assertion of formal class antagonisms results in a vitiated analysis of work relations, for a number of reasons. By asserting antagonisms it eliminates any need to investigate actual work-management relations. By imputing constant resistance and class consciousness it fails to attach importance to worker attitudes and motivations, regarding them as irrelevant. It thus leads to a conception of control which accords no significance to management efforts – by various devices – to generate some level of consent. This is the final shortcoming of Braverman's analysis of control, that it fails to regard control as a relationship; fails to grasp that for employers to be able fully to exploit employees requires some control not only over direction and levels of work, but over willingness to expend effort at all. In short Braverman, by remaining at the level of abstraction where relations between workers and capitalists can be described as formally antagonistic, fails to perceive the importance, to the employer, of this antagonism not becoming visible to the worker. For were it to do so, no control short of outright coercion would be feasible; and as Weber remarked, coercion is a highly inefficient form of work control.

Managerial strategies

The capitalist employer, then, is constantly faced with the potentially contradictory need both to exploit the work force and to recreate the conditions which make this exploitation possible. Precisely how this tension is resolved and the differential weight that is given to each aspect of control varies from firm to firm, from occasion to occasion, and from society to society. This raises the question of how we conceptualise these variations and aspects of control. In general it is useful to distinguish three elements of employer strategies – job design, the structure of control and the nature of the employment relationship (Littler, 1982, p. 47). The first refers to the principles by which work jobs are designed; for example, deskilled jobs under Taylorism *versus* the development of generalised semi-skilled work in Japan. The second refers to the manner and intensity with which this work is controlled; for example 'responsible autonomy' *versus* highly prescribed work as suggested by Friedman (1977), and earlier by Fox (1974), or through task control allied to payment systems, as under Taylorism, compared to ideological control mediated through small-group cooperation and pressure. The employment relationship varies largely in terms of the *dependency* of the employee on this relationship – i.e. the extent to which it establishes the dependency of the employee.

Dependency is determined by two sets of factors, namely alternative sources of need satisfaction and the capacity of workers to organise. In these terms the employment relationship clearly differs greatly between say, senior members of bureaucratic organisations such as universities, the civil service, the armed services, or commercial organisations, and shop floor employees, for whom the employment relationship offers little if anything beyond the cash nexus and the minimum protection and facilities established by law – and sometimes not even these.

Clearly an important factor in the dependency generated by the employment relationship is its scope and pervasiveness. By the pervasiveness of the employment relationship we refer to variation in the number of benefits which the employer contracts to supply, or accepts responsibility for supplying, or which the employee can reasonably be expected to receive, so long as performance and attitude are judged adequate. Organisations vary considerably in this respect (compare, for example, military organisations or the civil service with conventional industrial employers in Britain). More important are variations within organisations between management and shop-floor levels. It is these variations which largely but not wholly constitute the difference which Lockwood categorises in terms of work and market situation (Lockwood, 1958). Even more striking are differences in degree of pervasiveness of the employment relationship between different societies. Dore (1973) describes the typical Japanese employment system as one which accords to manual workers the privileges – fringe benefits, security, tenure, careers, etc. – which in Britain are only allocated to middle class employees. Weber's original formulation of bureaucracy represents not only a distinctive form of institutionalised control, but a distinct, and highly pervasive, form of employment relationship. Numerous writers have noted the significance of this form of employment for the generation of commitment (Dore, 1973, Edwards, 1979).

The work of Edwards, (1979) Friedman (1977) and others (see Wood, 1982) argues that management is able to manipulate these three levels of work structuration so as to construct a coherent strategy of control. The three levels are conceptually distinct. And while they have obvious implications for each other, they cannot simply be collapsed into each other. They refer to separate aspects of control and work organisation. However, the notion of strategy, now very widely used in analyses of work organisation, raises a number of points. First, it suggests some degree of purposiveness on the part of management, some degree of self-conscious deliberation. Second, it suggests that each strategy will represent a series of related positions on these three levels of structuration. A Taylorite approach to the division of labour could not co-exist with an emphasis on ideological control, as Fox (1974) has noted. Third, the notion of strategy implicitly rejects the suggestion of Braverman, that capitalism inevitably results in one major tendency in work organisation and control — i.e. deskilling and the elimination of worker autonomy, and the reduction of the employment relationship to the basic cash nexus.   If management can employ strategies of control, then it is clearly likely that such strategies will *vary* from plant to plant, from period to period, society to society. However, such variations themselves need to be explained: how far is management constrained in its choice of strategy? And what supplies the dynamic which constantly transforms these strategies?

The constraints on management strategy are both intrinsic to the history of particular management/worker relationships, and extrinsic, in that they emerge from the society's culture. For example, as Dore (1973) and Littler (1982) point out, the emphasis within Japanese work organisations on the values of familialism and nationalism, which plays an important part in wedding the employee's loyalty to the group to the values of the larger organisation, is only possible (at least to this extent) within a society with that particular pattern of history and culture. But such historical and cultural factors must not be over-emphasised, for apart from the danger of tautology — Japan is different because it is different — such an argument overestimates the extent to which any particular pattern of strategies was inevitable.

showed some trends towards paternalism and welfarism, often associated with Quaker employers. Early in the industrial period a number of industries and organisations, for example, the railways, dockyards, some brewers, lacking any clear conception of an 'appropriate' form of capitalist organisation or employment relationship, developed a highly dependent form of employment relationship, with internal promotion, the provision of pensions, health insurance, housing, recreational facilities, etc. But such possibilities, in the UK, were soon replaced by a minimised employment relationship, tight task control, and deskilled work — a pattern of institutionalised Taylorism the impact of which continues to dominate relations between management and workers.

But what of the dynamic which activates management's search for new, improved strategies? In general terms this dynamic is obvious: it is the possibility of worker resistance, of overt class consciousness. As Gintis has remarked, it is impossible to explain the (relatively) smooth functioning of a firm simply by reference to the explicit rules, work arrangements, procedures, etc. These owe their influence to the more basic fact that employee resistance to such constraints and directives has been diverted or eliminated. It is this process of constant tension between management intention, and potential or real employee resistance, which supplies the dynamic behind management's search for improved strategies. This is not to say that management is necessarily omniscient about available strategies, or able to foresee their consequences. Indeed British industrial development surely supplies a striking example of the manner in which short term gains can be achieved (through Taylorism) at the expense of a crippling escalation of management/worker mistrust and antagonism. Nor is it to suggest that management is self-consciously concerned with worker class attitudes. No, management deals with such priorities as waste, efficiency, staffing levels, availability of desired types of labour, ways of reducing dependency on potentially militant workers, new technology which can reduce bottlenecks and so on. But management's concern with these technical management issues of efficiency is also a concern with adjusting the balance of advantage in class relations between management and labour. Such concerns inevitably raise the managerial problems of how to effect the desired changes, how to avoid or short circuit worker resistance. These are strategic considerations.

Furthermore, the use of a particular strategy is both constrained by earlier strategies, and acts to limit future choices. Particular strategies exist within patterns of strategic response. This has been noted, for example, by Fox (1974) who argues that once a pattern of 'low-trust' relations has been established it is extremely difficult for management to be either willing or able to instigate a move towards 'high trust' relations. High discretion work roles – or those which involve 'responsible autonomy', are intended to maintain 'managerial authority by getting workers to identify with the competitive aims of the enterprise so that they will act "responsibly" with a minimum of supervision' (Friedman, 1977, p. 48). But such strategies are unlikely to work – and they are unlikely to be tried – on workers whose entire experience of management has led them to distrust management's intentions and practices, and who see relations with management as a contested terrain, where both sides constantly battle over the shifting frontier of control.

Recent writers – notably Friedman and Edwards – have suggested varieties of management strategy. Friedman distinguishes between Direct Control and Responsible Autonomy, Edwards between Technical Control and Bureaucratic Control.

Technical control 'involves designing machinery and planning the flow of work to minimise the problem of transforming labour power into labour as well as to maximise the purely physically based possibilities for achieving efficiencies' (Edwards, 1979, p. 112). Technical control is 'embedded' in technological organisations and work design. It clearly implies the form of control described by Friedman (and Braverman), but differs in that it is explicit not only about degree of discretion (which is low) but *where* and *how* the detailed control and direction of work occur.

Bureaucratic control, on the other hand, occurs through 'the social and organisational structure of the firm and is built into job categories, work rules, promotion procedures, discipline, wage scales, definitions of responsibilities, and the like' (Edwards, 1979, p. 131). Bureaucratic control is institutionalised control, exercised through the structure of the organisation, and is manifest in rules, procedures and regulations. In these ways bureaucratic control differs distinctly from technical control, in terms of the location of control and the manner of control.

But bureaucratic control differs from technical control in another, crucial way. It not only institutionalises control – and therefore, to some extent, conflict; it also provides definite structures of rewards and sanctions. Edwards is acutely aware that one of the attractions of the bureaucratic form of control is its pervasive nature: it offers a conception of employment which covers many more aspects of the employee's life and behaviour than technological control. In so doing of course, bureaucratic control represents an attempt, through the mobilisation of a particular conception of the employment relationship, and a particular location and manner of work control, to attract worker loyalty through positive sanctions, and through the establishment of a graded hierarchy of benefits available to 'responsible' and 'reliable' employees.

Edwards's analysis is a considerable improvement on Braverman's more rigid insistence on the significance of just one characteristic form of control under capitalism. Nevertheless it can be seen that Edwards, and to a greater extent Friedman, are more concerned to isolate forms of control in terms of large-scale empirical types than to isolate the various dimensions and mechanisms of control. The result is that the classifications offered sometimes contain not variation along the same dimensions, but different dimensions. The classifications are, broadly speaking, grounded in limited historical or empirical variation, not on an analysis of the requirements of employee control within capitalism. Yet it would seem that any classification of forms of control should, ideally, start with some consideration of these requirements, and how they are achieved, for only once this has been done is it possible to identify the varieties of control dimensions and mechanisms. As it is, there is a danger with descriptive classifications that they fail to grasp the variety of aspects of organisational control; that they focus on the 'formal', and official and ignore the informal aspects of control; and that they compare forms of control which are incomplete and therefore incomparable.

Both Friedman and Edwards, by failing to distinguish between the manner, location and form of direction of work, and efforts to ensure some level of consent or legitimation, and by not distinguishing between the control of work and the organisation of employment, construct typologies which are incomplete. This limitation is shown in two ways. First, both authors pay insufficient attention to the ways in which under Direct Control, or Technical Control, some level of consent is achieved. Without it even these explicit and detailed forms of control would be inadequate, as the following examples demonstrate. First, Ruth Cavendish (1982), in her account of working on a motor components assembly-line, falls under the illusion that the actual power to control work is vested in the line itself:

Its discipline was imposed automatically through the light, the conveyor belt and the bonus system. We just slotted in like cogs in a wheel. Every movement we made and every second of our time was controlled by the line; the chargehands and supervisors didn't even have to tell us when to get on. They just made people like Josey obey if they wouldn't buckle under. You couldn't really oppose the organisation of the work because it operated mechanically.

But she goes on immediately to say:

The bonus system and the line speed even led the women to discipline each other; getting 'up the wall' put out the person behind and we had informal arrangements to help avoid that. But these also ensured that we made up the right number of components so the supervisors' job was really done for them.

(ibid., p. 107.)

An identical contradiction is conveyed by Kamata (1982), describing the experience of working on the Toyota assembly lines in Japan. At first he expresses a simple notion of Technical Control:

The people working on the line are nothing more than power consumed in the process of assembly. What is achieved at the end of the line is the result of our combined energy. There's no need to shout at or berate workers to make them work. Just start the conveyor and keep it going: that's enough. The conveyor belt forces the workers into submission. During our working hours, we can't even talk. Even if we wanted to chat, the noise is so awful we can't hear one another.

(Kamata, 1982, p. 26.)

But shortly afterwards, Kamata recognises the impact and importance of workers policing each other:

... if Fukuyama, the worker on my right, falls behind, he'll pull me behind, since I barely keep up with the work myself. Even if Fukuyama finishes his job in time, should I take longer on my job, then the next worker, Takeda, will be pulled out of his position. It takes enormous energy to catch up with the line, and if things go wrong, the line stops. That means overtime. So we do our job in a hell of a hurry to keep our fellow workers from suffering. That is how Toyota raises output.

(Kamata, 1982, p. 48.)

These two examples, from totally different contexts, illustrate that even within the narrow confines of assembly-line work active compliance involving work group self-policing is essential for getting the work out, so that any understanding of 'control' needs to take account of such implicit interactions.

Secondly, like Braverman, Friedman, and to a lesser extent Edwards, by focusing on the labour process – the way in which shop-floor work is designed and controlled – ignore the possibility that control of the labour process may be achieved in ways which are not apparent at the point of production itself. This can occur through the organisation of the employment relationship, for example. It can also occur through selection procedures, preparatory training and socialisation, and other methods.

Discussions of 'strategies' of capitalist control tend to suffer, at least in recent debates, from an excessive interest in control as it appears in methods and techniques as they affect the worker at the point of production. This overlooks the possibility that control of work and work force can be achieved for the capitalist away from the point of production, indeed away from the organisation itself. Capitalists are not, after all, despite the insistence of some recent authors, interested in control *per se*. The first priority of capitalism is accumulation, not control. Control only becomes a concern when profitability is threatened.

Thirdly, it is not always easy or possible to separate control strategies, of whatever sort, and at whatever level of the organisation, from other, more technical decisions. One distorting legacy of Braverman is the assumption, not simply that control is achieved via one process – deskilling – and in one arena – the point of production – by one method – the increasing specification of work, but that a separation of control decisions from other decisions concerning levels and areas of investment, types of product and raw material, marketing strategies, accountancy procedures and so on is always clearly possible. In practice this distinction is not easy to establish.

At the level of the firm, an adequate classification of managerial strategies within the capitalist enterprise must move beyond description, beyond forms of control of and at the work process itself, to take cognisance of the distinctions suggested earlier between direction and consent, job design, control and employment. Such a classification must draw on the work of those writers who, in analyses of organisational structure, have noted more complex forms and mechanisms of control than those posited by recent writers on the labour process (see Salaman, 1979).

The achievement of consent

So far we have argued that control invariably and unavoidably contains two inter-related elements – specification and the achievement of consent – and that these elements are given differential attention and weight in forms of management strategy which occur at three discrete levels of structuration: job design, work control and the nature of the employment relationship. The next chapters will consider these issues in connection with current developments and tensions within the design of work and employment in the UK, paying particular attention to the nature of current technological developments and tendencies in work design. For the moment our attention is devoted to a consideration which has hitherto been left unexplored in this chapter: how is acquiescence achieved? We have seen that certain forms of management strategy – high trust, 'responsible autonomy', or Japanese practices – tend to generate legitimacy and 'trust'. Particular attention has been focused on the nature of the employment relationships. But these strategies alone do not supply all the answers. We must also consider the ideological dimension. First, however, some preliminary remarks are necessary.

First, in arguing the importance of ideology in encouraging working acquiescence, we must be careful not to exaggerate the ideology's causal significance. Ideologies do play some role, but their main importance is not in encouraging simple-minded 'false consciousness' among gullible workers, but in offering partial definitions of events which are supported by actual concrete circumstances and practices. Furthermore the role of ideology is not so much to encourage workers to see their role and the enterprise in terms favourable to management, but to undermine the possibility of alternative views of the enterprise. The prime function of ideology then is to establish the framework within which discussion of what is fair, reasonable, possible at work occurs.

Work-legitimating ideologies are closely dependent on work arrangements and experiences. From all points of view there is a sense in which legitimating conceptions of work have some basis in fact. For example, the notion that basically relations between management and worker are harmonious, except for errors of communication, or except where trouble-makers have encouraged dissension, is probably quite widespread. Its pervasiveness is not simply a result of media exhortation, or politicans' pronouncements: it also follows the very obvious *fact* of widespread co-operation and functional interdependence at work.

While it may be true that there is a fundamental conflict of interest between capital and labour, in *day-to-day* relations, workers, supervisors and managers work together in a real, functional interdependence, in practical co-operation. Furthermore, as many commentators point out, there is a real sense in which, while having opposed interests, workers and employers also have shared interests: in the success of their products, in competitive advantage, ultimately in the success of 'their' firm. It is these everyday realities of work within the capitalist firm which are seized on by ideologies of consensus and harmony. These ideas have a real, lived, basis. But they are partial; they focus on some aspects rather than others, and they define as abnormal and pathological another major element of work experience: conflict.

Secondly, work-legitimating ideologies operate not simply through their explicit emphases – many of which probably appear to be obviously propagandist – but through the assumptions which they carry. Characteristic assumptions, as will be described below, are: that conflict is unnecessary and pathological; that if it occurs it should, if it is legitimate, be settled through negotiation without any alteration in basic structures and hierarchies; that the given economic system, technology, management, etc.

are simply neutral – they cannot be changed, since they are required by a form of economy and society which is itself unchangeable and most advantageous to all citizens and workers.

As Westergaard and Resler remark: 'At the centre of the core assumptions of our society, clearly are the institutions of property and the market and the working premises which go with them....The core assumptions of our society are firmly in line with the interests of one small group. That group comprises top business and large property owners.' (Westergaard and Resler, 1975, pp. 249, 251.) Earlier these authors have forcibly made the point that is being repeated here: that power is inherent in anonymous social mechanisms, that it derives from the routine workings of unchallenged assumptions, that the institutionalisation of conflict is a key example of the significance of shared assumptions, which supply the 'rules of the game' within which conflict is played out without threatening the basic structure (Westergaard and Resler, 1975, p. 147).

In general, ideologies contain a structure of related ideas, which are significant not only separately but in their totality and in the series of inter-related assumptions which they carry. For example, work-legitimating ideologies contain a number of themes. At one level, there is the extent to which the over-arching form of economy itself – capitalism – with what are regarded as its consequences for economic decision-making, the imperatives of the market and so on, is regarded as acceptable, or inevitable. Of a similar level of generality, but with even greater significance for employees' attitudes towards detailed aspects of organisational hierarchy and decision-making, are ideologies of technocracy, with their attendant insistence on the neutrality and inevitability of modern, scientific, rational, technologies and social structures. Also at a very high level of generality, are cultural norms which assert the legitimacy of property rights in the enterprise. In principle, the right of the employer to own and sell the product is not generally challenged in Western economies. Four hundred years of surveillance, coercion and moralising have inculcated the legitimacy of property rights, so that British capitalists are not faced with the open 'pilfering' at every stage of the production process which occurs in many Third World economies where obligations to family and kin take precedence over obligations to impersonal, bureaucratic work organisations.

At a more detailed and specific level are those notions which may be described as characteristically managerial ideologies. These have a number of elements. The first priority of any such ideological effort is to demonstrate the importance of the managerial function – to establish the role of management within the differentiated enterprise, and to show that it is necessary, as an organisational function. Furthermore, once the abstract requirement for management is established, managerial ideologies seek to stress the characteristics and rarity of the useful and efficient manager. This can be done by reference to a number of ideas – as Bendix and Child report

(Bendix, 1974, Child 1969). Managers themselves, and their spokesmen, spend time and effort seeking to establish the abstract need for management in the modern enterprise, and to justify the differential rewards which managers receive – usually by reference to individual achievement of rare skills and knowledge necessary for the execution of demanding technologically-based functions.

Numerous writers have testified to the importance of this aspect of management in practice (Benyon, 1973) and in principle (Bendix, 1974, Child, 1969). Child, for example, plots how British managers were originally faced with problems of legitimacy and how these were gradually transformed into technical problems of efficiency. Clearly these two aspects are closely interlocked, at least in recent history. The major legitimation of current management is precisely in its claim to an unique and critical competence (Offe, 1976). Interestingly, as Burawoy (1978) has pointed out, one of the important implications of Taylorism was that by separating design and execution it established clearly, and for the first time, the necessity of management contributions to production. Management could no longer be regarded as superfluous, since if Taylorist systems were installed, production was now impossible without management's co-ordinating and design functions.

The other side of this particular coin was the transformation from a populist conception of labour to a managerialist view. Under nineteenth century modes of work control the workers saw themselves as the sole creative factor in production. In the USA, and to a lesser extent in Britain, Taylorism and the rationalisation movement generally undermined the populist view of labour and substituted a conception of labour as a passive factor of production, a mere appendage of the machine (Palmer, 1975, p. 44).

The establishment of management as a separate function, distinct from shop floor workers, with unique expertise and responsibilities, and with major and critical claims to authority over the shop floor upon which the efficiency of the whole enterprise depends (except in times of recession or economic difficulty when external, uncontrollable factors are held responsible), is a crucial first step in the establishment of control over the workforce. This is not because management as described then designs the functions of the deskilled workers. It is because once this conception of management has been accepted by workers, they have, in effect, abdicated from any questioning of, or resistance to, many aspects of their domination. They have accepted the normality of their subordination. Resistance, when and if it occurs, will be largely about details. The important aspects, the hierarchical nature of the enterprise, the location of decisions, capital investment, etc., have effectively been removed from the agenda.

Any of these levels of legitimation may be successful, even if in particular cases workers reject managers' right to manage, criticise their competence, pilfer, question their decision-making or seek to reduce differentials. The importance of notions and levels of legitimacy does not depend upon the achievement of a constantly deferential, acquiescent and obedient workforce. If it did it would clearly be invalid since these conditions have never been met. The importance of these efforts is that they supply, when successful, a moral backdrop against which particular circumstances are argued or are seen to be exceptional. They structure the way the world, and the enterprise, is perceived and known. They are the moral elements out of which the enterprise, with its hierarchy and divisions, is constructed, by establishing a number of features which are regarded as unchangeable.

These ideas clearly play an important part in the constant negotiations within each enterprise of the frontier of control. But this shifting pattern of accommodation cannot simply be derived from, or explained in terms of, levels of acceptance of general notions of technology, management ideology, and so on. The achievement of consent, of a *modus vivendi* between management and the shop-floor, also crucially depends upon the construction of definite trade-offs and interactions which, while they can generate an adequate level of worker acquiescence, may have little to do with generating, or reflecting, large-scale legitimations.

Thus we need to conceptualise the particular acceptance of hierarchical authority. This problematic of 'particular acceptance,' of day-to-day compliance, cannot be subsumed under the concept of legitimacy, nor treated simply as a level of legitimation. Consent is also achieved outside formal organisational procedures for establishing legitimacy, in what is usually described as the 'informal' structure of organisations.

This concept has been used within organisational analyses to refer to those patterns and relationships which occur in a systematic manner, and are not random or idiosyncratic, but which equally are not prescribed by formal regulation and specification, and indeed might occur in conflict with these. This area of organisational life has long fascinated researchers of work organisation. One major outcome of their research is the possibility that this informal aspect of organisational life may add considerably to employees' feelings of identification with, or commitment to, the enterprise. To explore this possibility we need to consider the way in which formal rules and specifications (the direction of work) are actually applied and operated in practice. We need to move beyond the formalism of their approach, which remains at the level of formal direction as required by the imperative of accumulation, to an analysis of how, in practice, managers and workers *use* these formal specifications so as to achieve some areas of discretion. It is likely that these areas of discretion, of negotiated freedom from rules and restraint, serve to generate some level of consent. (See, for example, Katz, 1973; Burawoy, 1979; Gouldner, 1954.)

In considering the limits of formal rationality it is important to remember that all rule-based authority structures depend upon the interpretation of rules, procedures etc., by middle-management and foremen. Gouldner's discussion of the 'indulgency pattern' in his *Patterns of Industrial*

Bureaucracy (1954) illustrates the way in which the implementation of rules may be so structured, by those with authority to enforce them, that their enforcement, or lack of enforcement, by foremen, can be part of an explicit effort to gain some measure of commitment among the work force. Gouldner notes that a rule may be more effective if it is not made explicit, or not enforced, since such 'indulgency' can generate a willingness of the workforce to pursue the spirit of the rule, and not the letter. Gouldner notes that the design and imposition of rules is a response to the withdrawal of commitment, which makes specification of effort necessary.

Furthermore, the orientation of foremen and departmental managers to the formal structure may be very different from that of senior management. Most crucially, foremen have no career stake in the operation of formal control systems, and often such systems are regarded as an externally-imposed nuisance.

Actual shop-floor behaviour and relationships must be seen not as *consequences* of the unilateral imposition by management on a passive work force of specifications and prescriptions, but as a two-way exchange in which an accommodation concerning the meaning and relevance of such prescriptions is achieved in exchange for some level of commitment to the existing distribution of authority, and to working objectives. As Elger has remarked in a useful summary of these processes echoing Burns, it is only through an analysis of the ways in which all levels of employees participate and play some part in modifying and interpreting formal, organisational controls and objectives that we can understand the relationship between senior organisational members' objectives and decisions and actual organisational outcomes. Similarly, it is only through these processes of adjustment of the formal specifications that we can understand the development of what are, from the shop floor's point of view, more congenial arrangements, which can then be regarded as, to some extent, stable patterns of accommodation (Elger, 1975.)

Finally, a level of acquiescence and working arrangements may be achieved at the frontier of control, by the development of various informal games, routines and patterned exchanges. Numerous writers have noted the existence, in work places, of such patterned routines (Roethlisberger and Dickson, 1964; Roy, 1973; and Burawoy, 1979). These routines frequently revolve around the achievement by workers of what are held to be 'proper' levels of output. As Burawoy suggests, one outcome of such negotiations is that '...participation in games has the effect of concealing relations of production at the same time as coordinating the interests of workers and management. ...Playing the game generates the legitimacy of the conditions that defines its rules and objectives.' (Burawoy, 1979, p. 271-2.) Other structured negotiations within established rules and procedures and between clearly demarcated parties, in various forms of industrial relations, also serve to reinforce the parameters of discussion and the respective rights and responsibilities of each side.

The games which Burawoy and others have identified allow the emergence of a mutual *modus vivendi*, with management frequently pulling back from the enforcement of irksome rules, for ultimately the practising manager knows full well that: 'The power vested in the capitalist to structure the rules of the enterprise and to manipulate wage differentials and criteria of promotion and dismissal are insufficient to explain the enforcement of the labour exchange.' (Gintis, 1976, p. 45.) But these negotiations carry another message: that the structure of work emerges to some extent from the contributions of both parties – that the actual (as against formal) organisation of work does involve, and is based upon, dialogue, cooperation and inter-dependence. Thus everyday work negotiations supply concrete support to ideologies of harmony and consensus.

Conclusions

This chapter has ranged widely over issues of control at work. It was argued that the fully-developed factory system was slower to emerge than is generally realised, in such a way that control problems were postponed. When modern forms of work organisation did become predominant there were severe problems of coordination arising from the increasing division of labour, task-discontinuous organisation and the need to develop a new time orientation. But the problems of coordination were difficult to separate from the capital/wage labour relationship.

This raised the question of the capital/labour relation. What is 'capitalist' about capitalist work organisation? It was argued that though conflict is structured into the capital/labour relationship, nevertheless there is a dual nature to that relationship such that all labour processes depend on some level of 'consent' or compliance. In addition, abstract assertions of class antagonisms do not feed through in an unmediated way to concrete events or situations.

A major concern of this chapter has been to distinguish aspects of control and the three major forms of work structuration. Forms of management strategy all aim at maximising both aspects of control through the manipulation of the three forms of work structuring. Particular attention has been paid to the significance of some level of employee acquiescence at work, and the relationship between the inherent 'incompleteness' of all forms of work control and the inevitable centrality of workers' subjectivity for employers. Various mechanisms by which a sufficient level of acquiescence could be achieved were considered, with particular attention being paid to the role of the nature of the employment relationship, and ideological factors. It was stressed however that ideological factors gained their greatest purchase through their connection with concrete aspects of everyday work life – particularly with the fact of constant processes of mutual adjustment, games-playing, negotiation and cooperation.

This chapter has raised one major issue which will constitute the focus of the next chapter. In view of the elements and levels within management control strategies, what management strategies are currently being deployed within British industry? What tensions and contradictions are apparent within and between levels and aspects of these strategies? And what is the role of recent technological and job design innovations in the relationship between employer and employee?

5 · The Design of Jobs

This chapter continues our overall concern with 'class at work', with a consideration of recent developments in work design. Earlier chapters argued that class impinges on work through (a) the empirical, distributive inequalities which make up class differences in life chances, many of which are work-based; (b) through the operation of class interests and pressures – most important of which are those pressures which act upon capitalists' need to conduct and design their enterprises profitably – to achieve their interest against other class interests; and (c) through the continual, unresolved existence of tensions and contradictions in class relations between managers and managed, contradictions which derive from an opposition of interests occurring within a context (the enterprise) of co-operation and interdependence. Chapter 4 discussed, in some detail, the way in which this tension is articulated within the control relationship, as capitalists attempt to find a form of control which satisfies the opposing needs of direction, specification and regulation of a workforce which, to be most profitable, must be as amenable as possible to managements' requirements of level and intensity of effort, and at the same time, a form of control which is so relaxed and open as to encourage and channel worker commitment and participation. It is possible to see control strategies as oscillating between these two poles.

This chapter continues our interest in this basic work contradiction, through an exploration of movements and tendencies in work design. Chapter 4 outlined the relationship between control and efficiency. Here, we will consider criteria of work design, paying particular attention to the implications of these criteria for control of work.

Taylorism and the division of labour

The oldest economic principle of production is that of the division of labour. According to Adam Smith, the eighteenth century economist, the advantages of the sub-division of work are threefold: first, labour productivity increases because of enhanced specialised dexterity and 'skill'; second, there is a minimisation of changeover and work preparation time; third, decomposition of tasks stimulates the invention of specialised machinery. An engineer is faced not with a jumble of complex motions but with a limited set of repeated actions that he can reproduce by a machine

(Adam Smith, 1776). Charles Babbage, writing in 1832, considered this analysis to be incomplete and added the well-known Babbage Principle. Put simply, this involves stripping a skilled job to an essential core and deskilling all the surrounding tasks. This division is then linked to status and pay differences (Babbage, 1832.). The economic dynamic to this continued re-division of labour is labour cheapening, a process which is assisted by the reduction in the learning time for jobs and by weakening the bargaining power of workers.

Productive work involves both mental and manual labour, and what neither Adam Smith nor Babbage conceptualised clearly was that the job specialisation and narrowing which they advocated could be used to divide mental from manual labour. But twentieth century methods of production tend continually to separate mental and manual labour, planning and doing. As factories have increased in size, so planning of productive processes has been taken out of the workshop and placed in auxiliary planning and design departments.

Frederick Taylor's scheme of so-called 'scientific management', put forward in the 1890s, rests upon the principle of the division of mental and manual labour. In addition Taylorism (as it became known) involved:

1 A general principle of the maximum decomposition of work tasks.

2 The divorce of direct and so-called 'indirect' labour, by which was meant all setting up, preparation and maintenance tasks.

3 The minimisation of the skill requirements of any task, leading to minimum job-learning times.

In general, Taylor argued that the full possibilities of scientific management 'will not have been realized until almost all of the machines in the shop are run by men who are of smaller calibre and attainments, and who are therefore cheaper than those required under the old system.' (Taylor, 1903, p. 105.)

If we define Taylorism carefully, it is possible to contrast it with other forms of work organisation – the wave of labour rationalisation between 1890 and 1914 based on ideas developed in the British armaments industry; the systematic rationalisation entailed by Fordism in which flow production required the redesign of the whole factory (see below); and the bureaucratisation of the employment relationship, involving institutionalised career systems as in the post office and railways.

This contrast with other forms of work organisation raises the question of the extent of the influence of Taylorism. Our answer to this question is complex (life is never simple!), so we will baldly state our conclusion and then proceed to qualify it. In general the direct and indirect influence of Taylorism on factory jobs has been extensive, so that in Britain job design and technology design have become imbued with a neo-Taylorism.

However, the line of influence was not straightforward, so that it is necessary to add several qualifications:

1 In Britain there was a time-lag of influence. Indeed, before 1914 the employers rejected 'American methods of management'.

2 Because of this time-lag it was *neo*-Taylorite systems which were eventually introduced, especially the Bedaux system. This combined Taylorism with the First World War fatigue studies and some elements of industrial psychology.

3 The Bedaux system was probably the most important channel for the spread of Taylorite ideas in Britain, but there were other channels, notably the transfer of American mass production industries associated with the emergence of multi-nationals.

4 There continued to be significant worker, supervisor and managerial resistance to Taylorism resulting in uneven adoption even within the mass production industries.

5 There is the curious paradox that despite the influence of Taylorism on job design, it did not succeed as a managerial *ideology* in Britain, unlike the USA. This paradox arose from the timing and context of implementation.

(For more detailed discussion of the above points see Littler, 1982).

Not all economies accepted Taylorite ideas of job design. A different pattern is exemplified by Japan. In Japan, partly because of the timing and rapidity of industrialisation, no extensive tradition of industrial craftsmanship was ever established. Instead Japanese factories depended on a tradition of work teams incorporating managerial functions and maintenance functions, with few staff specialists. There was a lack of job boundaries and continued job flexibility, unlike the prescriptions of Taylorism.

But in the United States and, more slowly, in Britain Taylorism, with its underlying principles of job fragmentation, tight job boundaries, and the separation of mental and manual labour, became the predominant ideal for job design. However, in practice there are limits to the division of labour implied by Taylorism. As Adam Smith realised, the division of labour depends on the desired volume of output, which, in turn, depends on the extent of the market. If a certain piece of work involved ten operations it would not be economical to employ a specialised, detailed worker for each operation if the total volume of output only required the time of one person. Thus, decomposition of tasks and Taylorite principles depend on mass markets, mass production and the velocity of throughput.

Fordism

This linkage of the division of labour and mass markets was realised clearly by Henry Ford. He largely established, captured and maintained a mass market for automobiles between 1908 and 1929, when the last of over 15 million Model T cars rolled off the assembly line. By that date the USA had about 80% of the cars in the entire world, a ratio of 5.3 people for every car registered, at a time when cars were a comparative luxury in Britain (Flink, 1975, pp. 67 and 70).

The model of production worked out by Ford between 1908 and 1913, to serve this mass market, presupposed the major principles of Taylorism, but went further in the transfer of traditional skills from workers to specialised machines. By 1914 about 15,000 machines had been installed at the vast new Highland Park plant and company policy was to scrap machines as fast as they could be replaced by improved types. In addition, Ford perfected the flow-line principle of assembly work. This means that instead of workers moving between tasks, the flow of parts is achieved as much as possible by machines (conveyors and transporters) so that assembly workers are tied to their work position and have no need to move about the workshop. A crucial consequence is that the pace of work is controlled mechanically and not by the workers or supervisors.

Associated with the new fixed-speed moving assembly lines was an accelerated division of labour and short task-cycle times. Ford pushed job fragmentation to an extreme. For example, in 1922, Henry Ford records a survey of jobs in his plants:

> The lightest jobs were again classified to discover how many of them required the use of full faculties, and we found that 670 could be filled by legless men, 2,637 by one-legged men, two by armless men, 715 by one-armed men, and ten by blind men. Therefore, out of 7,882 kinds of job...4,034 did not require full physical capacity.

(Ford, 1922, p. 108)

Having developed a new industrial technology based on the flow-line principle and extreme job fragmentation, Ford found that control of the production process was not equal to control of the workforce. Worker rejection of the new work processes was expressed in high rates of turnover, absenteeism and insufficient effort. For example, the head of Ford's employment department in 1913 cited a figure of $38 to train up a new worker: a small amount, but with an annual turnover of more than 50,000 workers (i.e. 400%) the total cost was two million dollars (Russell, 1978, p. 40; also Meyer, 1981).

The control techniques developed by Ford in response to these worker problems serve to mark off Fordism from Taylorism. One of Taylor's close associates asserted that he did not 'care a hoot what became of the workman after he left the factory at night; so long as he was able to show up the next morning in a fit condition for a hard day's toil' (Copley, 1915, p. 42). But Ford went outside the factory gates in an attempt to re-mould working-class culture in accordance with industrial discipline and efficiency. The so-called 'Five Dollar Day' offered workers large material incentives for altering their private lives as well as their work behaviour. A worker's bonus, access to company loans and, ultimately, his job depended on satisfactory personal habits (including no consumption of alcohol or tobacco). Home conditions and off-work behaviour were all investigated by the company's 'Sociological Department'! The Five Dollar Day was backed up by the

Americanisation programme, directed at immigrants and providing not only language instruction but also moral education into American, middle-class values (see Meyer, 1981.)

At the level of job design the effects of the introduction of the assembly line at Fords on productivity and profits is indicated by the fact that it reduced the time of chassis assembly from $12\frac{1}{2}$ hours to 2 hours 40 minutes (Flink, 1975, p. 77). Fine for the consumer but what does it mean for the producer? An idea of the pressures of mechanical control and of Fordism in practice is vividly conveyed in the following picture of work on the Citroen line in the 1970s:

> The crash of a new car body arriving every three or four minutes marks out the rhythm of the work.
>
> As soon as the car has been fitted into the assembly line it begins its half-circle, passing each successive position for soldering or another complementary operation, such as filing, grinding, hammering...it's a continuous movement and it looks slow: when you first see the line it almost seems to be standing still, and you've got to concentrate on one actual car in order to realise that car is moving, gliding progressively from one position to the next. Since nothing stops, the workers also have to move in order to stay with the car for the time it takes to carry out the work. In this way each man has a well-defined area for the operations he has to make, although the boundaries are invisible: as soon as a car enters a man's territory, he takes down his blowtorch, grabs his soldering iron, takes his hammer or his file, and gets to work. A few knocks, a few sparks, then the soldering's done and the car's already on its way out of the three or four yards of this position. And the next car's already coming into the work area. And the worker starts again. Sometimes, if he's been working fast, he has a few seconds' respite before a new car arrives: either he takes advantage of it to breathe for a moment, or else he intensifies his effort and 'goes up the line' so that he can gain a little time, in other words, he works further ahead, outside his normal area, together with the worker at the preceding position. And after an hour or two he's amassed the incredible capital of two or three minutes in hand, that he'll use up smoking a cigarette, looking on like some comfortable man of means as his car moves past already soldered, keeping his hands in pockets while the others are working. Short-lived happiness: the next car's already there: he'll have to work on it at his usual position this time, and the race begins again, in the hope of gaining one or two yards, 'moving up' in the hope of another peaceful cigarette. If, on the other hand, the worker's too slow, he 'slips back', that is, he finds himself carried progressively beyond his position, going on with his work when the next labourer has already begun his. Then he has to push on fast, trying to catch up. And the slow gliding of the cars, which seems to me so near to not moving at all, looks as relentless as a rushing torrent which you can't manage to dam up:

eighteen inches, three feet, thirty seconds certainly behind time, this awkward join, the car followed too far, and the next one already appearing at the usual starting point of the station, coming forward with its mindless regularity and its inert mass. It's already halfway along before you're able to touch it, you're going to start on it when it's nearly passed through and reached the next station: all this loss of time mounts up. It's what they call 'slipping' and sometimes it's as ghastly as drowning.

(Linhart, 1981, pp. 15-16)

A strikingly similar account to Linhart's is provided by Satoshi Kamata, describing the work experience in a Japanese car factory:

I have really been fooled by the seeming slowness of the conveyor belt. No one can understand how it works without experiencing it. Almost as soon as I begin, I am dripping with sweat. Somehow, I learn the order of the work motions, but I'm totally unable to keep up with the speed of the line. My work gloves make it difficult to grab as many tiny bolts as I need, and how many precious seconds do I waste doing just that? I do my best, but I can barely finish one gear box out of three within the fixed length of time. If a different-model transmission comes along, it's simply beyond my capacity. Some skill is needed, and a new hand like me can't do it alone, I'm thirsty as hell, but workers can neither smoke nor drink water. Going to the toilet is out of the question. Who could have invented a system like this? It's designed to make workers do nothing but work and to prevent any kind of rest.

(Kamata, 1982, p. 22).

The answer of course, is that Ford invented the system, and as these examples from Citroen in France and Toyota in Japan indicate, Ford's competitors imitated his success and installed moving assembly lines with fixed speeds and short task cycles themselves. The factors which fuelled the diffusion of Taylorism and Fordism are considered in the next section.

Diffusion of Taylorism and Fordism

At least for the mass production industries, Taylorism and Fordism became the predominant ideals for organising work in the USA, Britain and many other economies. Two things helped the spread of the ideas and techniques. Firstly, the interwar years were characterised by the internationalisation of technology. In the newer industries, such as electrical engineering, chemicals and vehicles, this was particularly true. For example, one of the largest electrical engineering companies in the USA was Westinghouse Electric. This corporation became a strong advocate of Taylorism, time study and systematic job analysis. In 1924 Westinghouse concluded a technical exchange agreement with Siemens, one of the two largest German electrical firms, which extended the influence of Westinghouse management methods in German factories. Similarly, Mitsubishi Electric of Japan had a similar agreement with Westinghouse in the 1920s. The managing director of Mitsubishi went to the USA to study Westinghouse techniques and became a strong advocate of Taylorite time and motion studies (Levine and Kawada, 1980, p. 264).

Taylorism and Fordist techniques had of course to be adapted to the labour markets, economic conditions and culture of the receiving society. But one mechanism allowed direct transplants. The diffusion of American management and job design techniques was assisted by the mechanism of the multinational corporation. Ford established subsidiaries in Britain, Germany, Japan and other countries, as did Ford's main competitor – General Motors. Ford first moved to Britain as early as 1911 when the company bought an old car plant in Manchester, and the Dagenham factory, built in 1930-31, was the first major Ford plant outside the USA. Ford's example was followed by General Motors, who took over Vauxhall in 1925. When the General Motors takeover occurred the corporation radically reorganised the existing factory. All machines on the shop-floor were organised on the flow-line principle and assembly was done on moving tracks. Each department and assembly area was co-ordinated to produce one component every twenty minutes (Lewchuk, 1983, p. 96).

The multinational corporation allowed not only the transfer of techniques and machinery but of *people*, who brought with them an extensive knowledge of details and general orientations to mass production. For example General Motors brought over a small pool of American engineers who could train British engineers in the new techniques.

There were still, of course, differences between companies. Citroen of France started an assembly line for its first postwar model as early as 1919 and, lacking qualified engineers, the company later hired American engineers and brought them to Europe. The Austin car company in Britain introduced moving assembly lines between 1922 and 1925 at the Longbridge plant, whilst Morris Motors, perhaps the leading British car firm in the interwar years, delayed the reorganisation of manufacturing methods until 1934 (Fridenson, 1978).

In general, by the mid-1930s Taylorite techniques had spread across Europe whilst Fordism and the moving assembly line had penetrated the largest car firms and spread to other industries such as electrical engineering.

The Limits of Taylorism and Fordism

Even within the principles and practice of Taylorism and Fordism there are limits to job fragmentation and the transfer of skills to specialised machinery. First, there are the economic limits which we have already discussed – the decomposition of tasks depends on the velocity of throughput. Second, there are technical limits. Assume, for example, that in an engineering factory a given piece of work involves several operations such as planing, milling, turning and drilling. These various operations can be economically separated as the volume of throughput increases, each task being assigned to one man, or a group of men, who do nothing else. Thus, a worker may be assigned to drill a specific hole in each piece of metal. If the volume of work increases further, then a drilling fixture or jig may be used and the work of drilling may be further sub-divided by employing one man to put the parts to be drilled into the fixture and take them out again after the operation, and the other man to do the drilling and nothing else. This is an example of the divorce of direct and indirect labour discussed above. But without the further development of machining technology (which has not occurred until recently) it is difficult to sub-divide either of these functions further, no matter how big the market and the volume of output. In other words, the division of labour can be carried down to certain fundamental operations beyond which it must wait upon a transformation of the technology.

Thirdly, Taylorism and Fordism carry co-ordination and control costs. As the division of labour is extended, co-ordination measures must accompany such extension: for example, production planning, supervision and monitoring, and inspection procedures. This is not just a practical, managerial question but also a sociological question related to the development of industry. Early industrialisation in most economies, including Britain, depended on the use of existing forms of group or cultural solidarity and subordination, such as family and kin ties. Later patterns of work organisation, in eliminating such forms, left employers with stark and critical problems of harnessing labour's creative and productive powers. However, formal structures of control cost money and tend to offset gains from an extended division of labour. For example, many employers found that the clerical costs of installing and running Taylorite-type schemes were very high (Littler, 1982).

Fourthly, limits to the direct control methods of Taylor and Ford are set by increasing co-operation costs. If the linkages of workers to the work organisation are largely instrumental and entail very little commitment, then the purchase price of day-to-day worker compliance is inexorably increased during the upturn in the economic cycle when labour markets are tight. More broadly, Taylorite forms of work organisation are acceptable to employers only within certain types of product market. If price ceases to be the predominant factor in exchange, and non-price factors, such as reliability, quality and design, assume a larger significance, then this places a heavier emphasis on worker co-operation and worker commitment. In Taylorite/Fordist organisations workers are neither trained to show, nor are rewarded for, initiative. Here is an account by one American worker:

I am – or was – an American auto worker. I built GM cars for 16 years. Then, in March (1980), I was laid off indefinitely. ...It was not the worker who determines the quality of a car, but the executives in Detroit and the plant supervisors. The worker who performs a certain task 320 times a day, 5 days a week, knows more about the specifics of this particular job than anyone else. Yet, in 16 years, I have never been consulted on how to improve a job qualitatively or quantitatively. There are suggestion programs but their main concern is always 'how to save the company's money'. The auto worker can only build as good a car as he is instructed or permitted to build. We on the line take our cue from those in the head office. If they don't really care about the quality, they can't expect us to either.

(Douglas, 1980)

In this environment workers regard any demand for initiative or commitment as simply a bargaining counter in the struggles with supervisors and employers.

In Chapter 4 it was noted that since employment involves willingness to work in exchange for a wage, workers' subjectivity becomes an important element in the production process. These attitudes cannot be made irrelevant by any form of work control or discipline, however oppressive and onerous, so long as the work, however de-skilled or regulated, is done by humans. If they are relevant, then Taylorite forms of work design are likely to have extremely negative consequences for work attitudes. One characteristic response to this phenomenon is to install still tighter forms of work and control regulation (because the workers are so 'bloodyminded'); but as Fox and other writers have noted, this spiral of distrust, regulation, alienation, further distrust, and so on is often identified by management as unsatisfactory even from the point of view of management's practical, commercial priorities.

Job redesign in the 1970s

During the late sixties and early seventies, the apparent problems of technocracy and Taylorite strategies (organisational rigidity and inflexibility, the expansion of organisational complexity to handle fragmented work, the underutilisation of worker initiative, and numerous indicators of worker dissatisfaction) led to the emergence of a job redesign movement, largely based on industrial psychology, and a more broadly based Quality of Working Life (Q.W.L.) movement. The latter is conveniently symbolised by the 'Work in America' report (1973) and the report 'On the Quality of Working Life' (1973) in Britain (Wilson, 1973). These reports, and other writings, propound principles of 'good' job design which are the precise opposite of Taylorian principles. Typically, five have been put forward:

1 Principle of closure: the scope of the job should include all the tasks necessary to complete a product or process. Theoretically, the predicted result is that work acquires an intrinsic meaning and people can feel a sense of achievement.

2 Incorporation of control and monitoring tasks. Jobs should be designed so

that an army of inspectors is not required. The individual worker, or the work team, assumes responsibility for quality and reliability.

3 Task variety, i.e. an increase in the range of tasks. This implies a principle of comprehensiveness, which means that workers should understand the general principles of a range of tasks so that job rotation is possible.

4 Self-regulation of the speed of work and some choice over work methods and work sequence.

5 A job structure that permits some social interaction and perhaps cooperation among workers.

(See for example L. E. Davis, 1957 and 1966; Walton, 1979; Hackman and Oldham, 1975).

Through the 1970s these principles were the gospel of a few avant-garde consultants, and though there were isolated examples of new work systems, generally job design remained tied to traditional Taylorian principles. However, through the latter half of the 1970s and the early 1980s the pressure of – mainly Japanese – competition has forced many Western corporations to re-examine their philosophy of job design and control from a solid, down to earth perspective – that of profits.

The recent trends in job design cannot all be grouped together. As several authors have pointed out (Kelly, 1982; Savall, 1981), there have, in general, been three types: reorganisation of Fordist assembly lines, group technology, and job enrichment. We will consider each of these in turn.

Reorganisation of assembly lines

This type of job redesign has been concentrated in consumer industries, especially electrical appliances. Such changes have been associated with increased product variations in more competitive markets. Generally, depending on the type of product and the price structure, a large corporation needs at least two years to get back its investment of setting up a new mass production line. But, partly because of Japanese competition, the pace of change has quickened so that a comfortable cruise along a two year profit path has turned into a bumpy ride. It needs to be remembered that Fordist techniques are product-specific, involving specialised machinery and narrow skills which are not readily transferable. The result has been that mass production facilities have become excessively inflexible and a cost burden, as it becomes harder and harder to consolidate the mass production of a standard product.

Thus the product market pressure has been to create more flexible work forms able to accommodate more rapid product changes without creating an entirely new line (Sabel, 1982, p. 199). For example, in a large British electrical plant the old work system consisted of a fixed-speed straight assembly-line. Work was machine-paced with about 30 people doing one task each – wiring, soldering, assembly, or testing – with task cycles varying between 25 to 45 seconds. Workers could not leave their work stations for as long as one minute and if there was a breakdown or disruption at any point then the entire line stopped. The work re-design carried out in the 1970s consisted of introducing buffer inventories of partly processed goods between work stations and grouping all automatic operations together so that workers were de-coupled from the machine pace by these buffers (see Fig. 1). The line itself is not so highly mechanised, the jobs have been slightly enlarged and task cycles are approximately double that of the old line. But the crucial point was that though the initial investment costs of the new line were higher, capacity utilisation increased because of greater flexibility. The new work arrangements could adapt to product changes much faster and thus reduce overall unit costs.

Most of the redesign changes in assembly lines have still resulted in production processes with one-man work stations; often more cooperation between workers is possible (see Fig. 1), but it is not usually essential to the flow of production. We now turn to a form of redesigned work organisation which explicitly recognises the value of cooperative team work, namely group technology.

Figure 1. *Redesign of assembly lines*

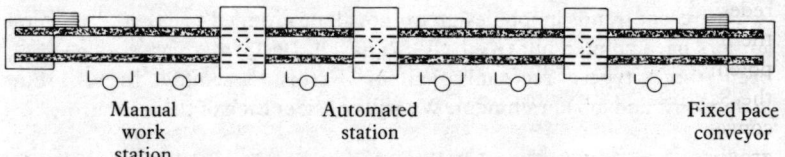

Manual work station   Automated station   Fixed pace conveyor

a. Conventional Ford-type assembly line with machine-pacing.

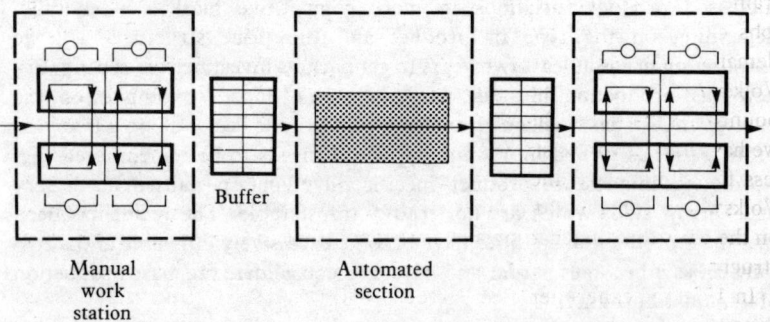

Manual work station   Automated section

b. Redesigned assembly line, with automated operations grouped together, and workers de-coupled from the machine pace by buffers.

Group technology

Group technology represents a realisation by some employers of the value of work groups as a basis for work organisation, because it enables them to move beyond the cash nexus and tap the artesian sources of team-work, group problem-solving and mutual social control. These groups have been tried in mass production industries such as car manufacture in Sweden and Germany; for example, Volkswagen started experimenting with them at its new Salzgitter engine plant in 1975. Normally car engines are built on a conventional fixed speed assembly line with task cycles of about one or two minutes. Instead, Volkswagen began a small scale experiment with four groups of seven workers (two teams on each shift). Within the groups four men worked on assembly, two did testing and one man was in charge of materials. The entire group was de-coupled from the machine-paced line but had to meet a quota of seven engines per team per day. The workers received special training so that they could do all the team jobs and were free to rotate job assignments as they wished. Each group had a team leader (*Gruppensprecher*) who was responsible for liaison with management, and foremen were eliminated (D. Jenkins, 1978).

The results of the Volkswagen experiment highlighted two overlapping problems of such work groups, which have recurred in different situations and economies. First, semi-autonomous workgroups run up against the existing power-balance between labour and capital. Employers see such job redesign as an opportunity to undercut the union in the workplace, whilst the unions tend to be opposed to informally elected workgroup leaders as potential usurpers of union influence. This conflict of interests occurred at the Salzgitter plant with the eventual outcome that the team leaders were converted into shop stewards, and foremen were brought back to oversee the groups as Volkswagen wanted to prevent the erosion of management power.

Apart from the issue of autonomous groups as a threat to the existing structures of shopfloor power, there was the question of how the specially trained team workers fitted into the skill and wage hierarchy. The enlarged jobs caused a union/management dispute over wage levels. The unions demanded that the workers should be paid at a skilled rate which Volkswagen resisted. In effect, this re-combination of tasks across Taylorian boundaries disrupted the Babbage Principle of labour cheapening which, as we have said, involves stripping a skilled job to an essential core and paying less for all ancillary and servicing tasks performed by unskilled workers. Volkswagen concluded that they did not want masses of re-skilled workers on the basis that they had no jobs for them — they did not fit into the normal structure.

In 1978 the experiment was ended. Volkswagen management considered the system too costly and that it was not possible to fill the factory with the 'dreams of another world' (D. Jenkins, 1978, p. 20).

The Volkswagen case is important. It exemplifies the major theme of this chapter, and in a sense of the book as a whole: the inherent instability of any particular management strategy as an effort to resolve the basic tension between the need for control and the need for participation as played out against a backdrop of competitive market pressures, technological developments and management/workers (i.e. class) relations. The Volkswagen experiment failed, partly at least, for the sorts of reasons given by General Motors' Director of Employee Research and Training at its Chevrolet division. He remarked that: '...the subjects of participation are not necessarily restricted to those few matters that management considers to be of direct, personal interest to employees...(A plan cannot) be maintained for long without (a) being recognised by employees as manipulative or (b) leading to expectations for wider and more significant involvement − "Why do they only ask us about plans for painting the office and not about replacing this old equipment and rearranging the layout?" Once competence is shown (or believed to have been shown) in say, rearranging the work area, and after participation has become a conscious, officially sponsored activity, participators may very well want to go on to topics of job assignment, the allocation of rewards, or even the selection of leadership. In other words, management's present monopoly of control can in itself easily become a source of contention.' (quoted in Edwards, 1979, p. 156).

In general, mass production industries have proved to be a hostile milieu for group technology. In batch production the story has been more complex. It is still the case that the vast majority (up to 80%) of engineering components are produced in batches of less than 1,000. This is significant because traditional batch production costs between ten to thirty times more than mass production of an item. This is because of the need to continually re-set the machines and the considerable delays in the movement of components between machines. Most items spend long periods collecting dust on the factory floor queueing for the next process.

In looking at batch production in the early 1970s, Turner noted that it is complex, because succeeding batches require different machining operations in different sequences. This entails a large amount of variety and great uncertainties (look at the work flow pattern between different machines in Fig. 2 overleaf). Associated with this complex pattern is a lack of complete knowledge of the production system by management, so that instead of a production planning programme there is a monitoring of work-in-progress by an army of progress-chasers and harassed foremen (Turner, 1970).

In the early 1960s one solution to these problems was the evolution of so-called 'group technology'. This originally was a technical term referring to a new lay-out of production based on grouping together all the machines necessary to complete a particular type of component (see Fig. 2). This in turn was based on classification of all components, standardisation as far as possible and grouping the components into 'families'. It improved machine utilisation and it speeded up the throughput of work by simplifying work flow.

Figure 2. *Work flow in batch production*

a. Typical 'Functional Layout' and work flow

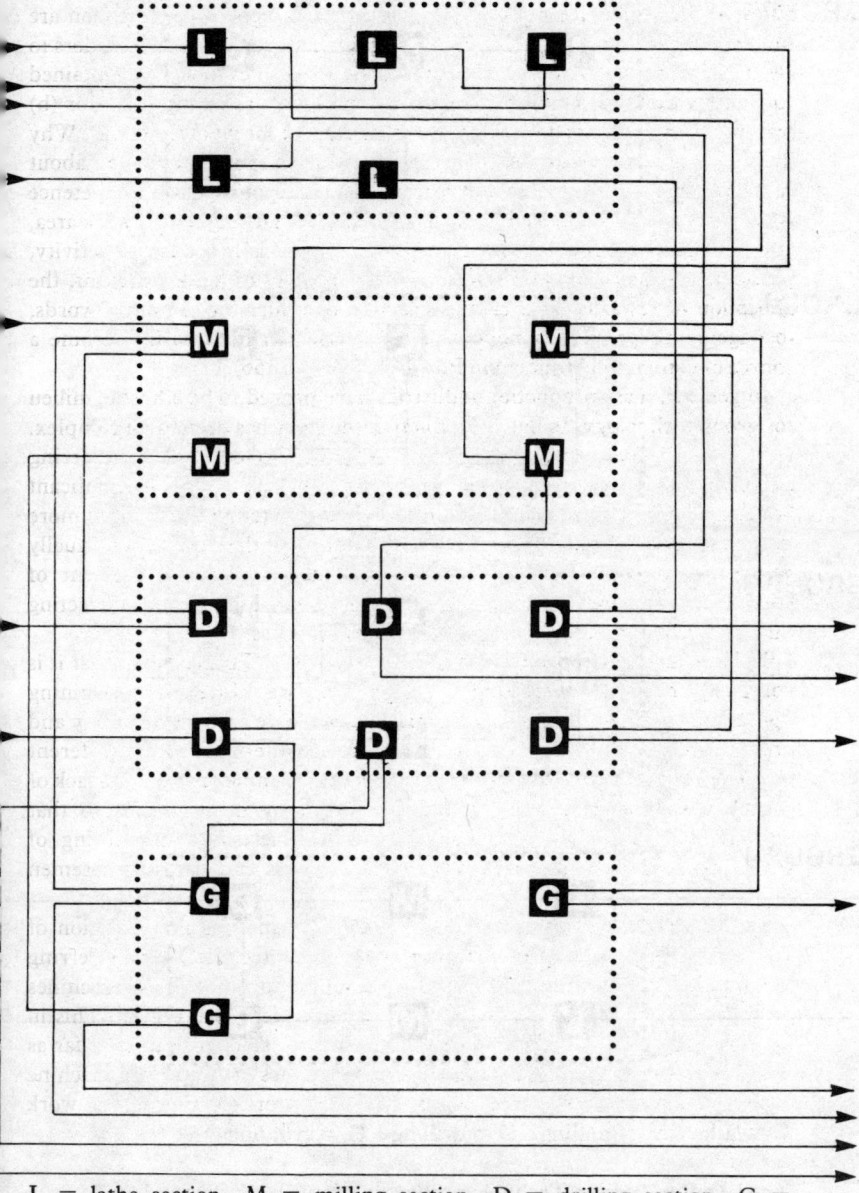

L = lathe section   M = milling section   D = drilling section   G = grinding section

The conventional Functional Layout means a complex work flow and a high volume of work in progress

b. Typical 'Group Layout' and work flow

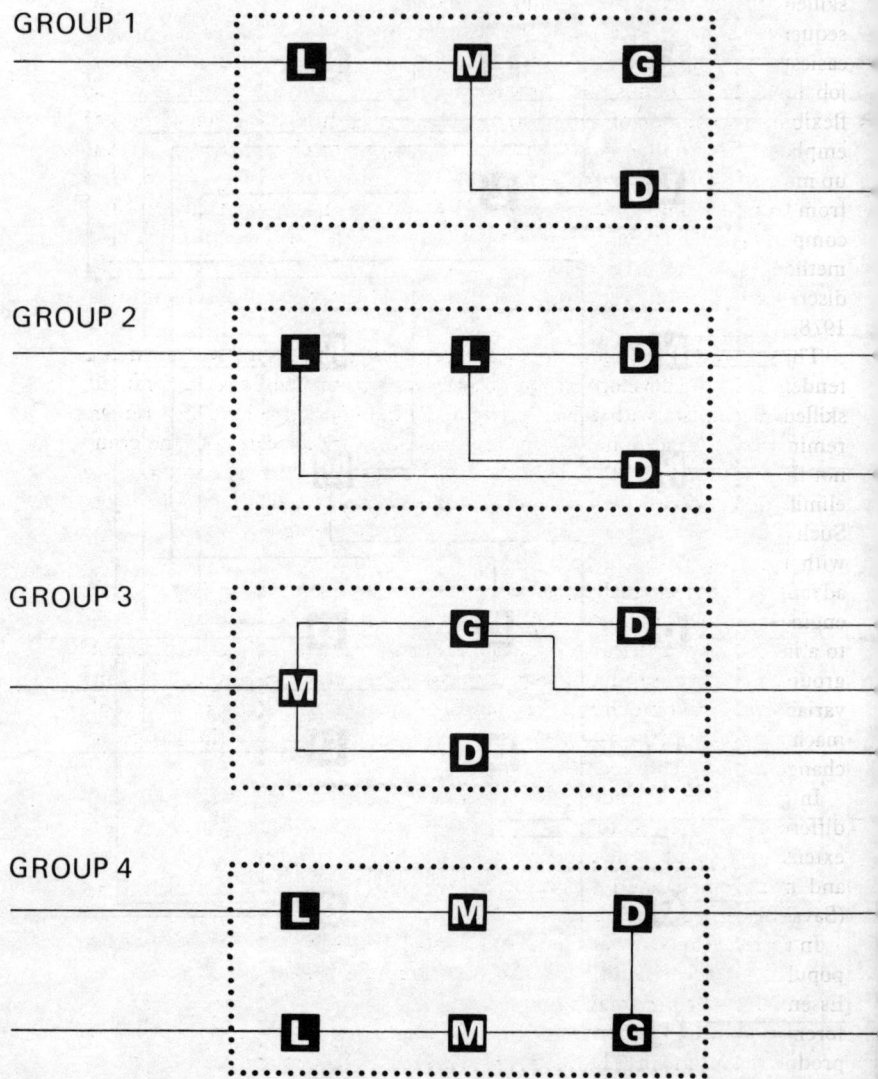

L = lathe   M = milling   D = drilling   G = grinding

The layout for Group Technology allows a simple work flow and
low volumes of work in progress

But in creating a cellular work structure, engineering employers also created new work groups. At first this received no explicit attention, but as skilled machinists' dissatisfaction with their loss of discretion over the sequence of work increased (the machinists could no longer choose the easiest job first, or the safest job when they were tired, or the most lucrative job in terms of bonus) and as employers recognised the potential of job flexibility, the notion of semi-autonomous work groups was given increasing emphasis. This potential was based on machine 'stretch-out', that is, setting up more machines than workers, and re-training so that workers could move from lathe to drilling machine to grinder. But beyond this stretch-out some companies have given the new work groups some discretion over work methods and job assignments, secure in the knowledge that worker discretion is severely restricted by the control built into the system (Green, 1978, p. 18).

Thus, group technology in batch producing industries has created a tendency for the development of flexible work groups based on generalised, skilled machinists with a lack of rigid job boundaries. There is a return, reminiscent of traditional internal contract, of work allocation to the group not the individual (Littler, 1982). Insofar as charge-hands and foremen are eliminated, this reduces control and coordination costs to the employer. Such groups also increase worker adaptability and enable the team to cope with the absences of any of its members. But whatever the managerial advantages of group technology, after a limited spread to about 10% of batch engineering firms in the early and mid-1970s, the process of diffusion came to a halt. This was because the information burden of setting up a reliable group technology production system was too great — there were too many variables and too much unpredictability. Now, with the spread of flexible machining centres and cheaper shop-floor minicomputers the pattern of change will probably accelerate.

In general, the introduction of flexible work groups has occured in very different industrial sectors and in firms varying in size and technology. The extension of small-scale experiments has often been opposed by both unions and management, and the diffusion of such groups is still very limited (Savall, 1981, pp. 69-71 and 98-101).

In recent years one variant of autonomous shop-floor groups has become popular, namely Quality Control (Q.C.) circles. What are Q.C. circles? Essentially they are small groups of workers (about 5-20), usually led by a foreman or senior worker, who meet regularly to study and solve all types of production problems. In addition such groups are intended to stimulate motivation and involvement on the shop-floor. Unlike earlier human relations ideas, Q.C. circles involve systematic training of shop-floor workers and access to technical assistance to solve problems.

The original idea of Q.C. circles was American: the basis being the notion of improved worker motivation through employee participation in the decision-making process. The concept was transplanted to Japan in the

1950s, where it was adopted and re-worked by several management theorists, particularly Kaoru Ishikawa. The ideas gained popularity in Japan in the 1960s and early 1970s and were re-cycled to the West in the later 1970s, surrounded by the aura of Japanese productivity and economic success. At present (1982) about 450 corporations in the USA and Canada make extensive use of Q.C. circles and about 200 firms in Britain have experimented with them, most notably Rolls Royce. Such ideas have never been totally absent from British shop-floors. The idea of 'briefing groups' designed to bring workers, supervisors and senior managers together to discuss 'common problems' is perhaps more familiar in the British context, but is clearly allied to the Q.C. concept (Hull, 1978, p. 35).

Given that Q.C. circles are *not* the same thing as work groups, what effects have they had, or are likely to have, on job design? The main effect is to bridge the mental/manual divide inherited from Taylorism. Q.C. circles tend to break with the traditional practices and assumptions implicit in most Western managerial control systems. Firstly, there is the assumption of high commitment to the work organisation, so that workers will devote time and effort, even outside work hours, to the analysis of work-related problems. Associated with this, Q.C. circles involve workers (at least in theory) in a genuine study process, requiring company resources and training. Furthermore, study groups are, after management vetting, provided with the means to institute new work practices in order to overcome the problems of productivity and quality.

All of this contrasts sharply with the conventional Taylorite assumption that workers know how to increase productivity or ensure quality but are holding back for no justifiable reason – that worker indifference or even sabotage are the normal problems that management has to face and overcome. Indeed Taylor's starting-point was the pervasiveness of what he called 'soldiering', that, is a deliberate collective slow-down (Taylor, 1903, p. 30). Similarly, conventional factory suggestions schemes maintain the mental/manual divide by assuming that any useful suggestions will be analysed and implemented by management personnel.

One interesting example of the introduction of Q.C. circles in the West is that of Ford. The Ford Corporation, frightened of Japanese competition, decided in 1980 to implement the system in all its 25 manufacturing and assembly plants in Western Europe, involving all 140,000 shop-floor workers. The overall programme in 1980-81 was called 'After Japan'. Ford's stated objectives were to improve the quality of its products, reduce scrap, and encourage worker involvement. The unstated objectives were (probably) to increase labour productivity and change manning levels and traditional work practices (*The Financial Times,* 9 May 1980; *The Guardian,* 11 June 1980).

Ford followed the Japanese pattern of Q.C. circles, with some interesting differences. Each of its Q.C. groups consisted of 8-15 people, including a supervisor plus a representative from the quality control department. The reason for the inclusion of the latter is that the Taylorian inheritance has meant that production problems and quality control are the responsibility of staff departments divorced from the shop-floor, whereas in Japan the production worker, with his foreman, is much more responsible for checking the quality of his own work before it moves on down the line.

Another difference from the Japanese situation is that in Japan the labour force is all-Japanese, young and relatively well-educated. At Ford the circles often consist of a mixture of West Indians, Asians and Southern Europeans as well as English workers. The first thing that the circles demonstrated as forums of communication was that the traditional managerial methods of communication — posters and job instructions — often meant different things to different ethnic groups!

The attempted rushed adoption of Japanese Q.C. circles by Ford aroused the opposition of the main union — the Transport and General Workers Union. Rank and file union leaders complained that all changes in working practices should be discussed and mutually agreed with the union, and that the proposals cut across existing union structures (*The Financial Times,* 9 March and 25 April 1981). The outcome is that so far Q.C. circles have not been introduced in British Ford plants, but have spread across the rest of the European plants. Other British firms, such as Rolls Royce, have had more success in introducing Q.C. circles but the overall impact of this form of 'Japanisation' has yet to be determined.

Job enrichment

Job enrichment has generally involved a reorganisation of hierarchically-structured tasks, so that lower level jobs expand their areas of discretion. This form of job re-design has been more talked about than acted upon and generally it has been confined to white-collar workers, especially in the financial sector (see Herzberg, 1966 and 1976). In relation to shop-floor workers, 'job-enrichment' has usually meant the amalgamation of direct and indirect labour tasks such as setting up or maintenance, though even this limited step is contrary to strict Taylorite principles. Many shop-floor job enlargement experiments consist of re-combining a set of unskilled tasks in order to solve managerial problems of work-load balance and quality control. The effects are neatly summed up in a well-known statement of one chemical worker:

> You move from one boring, dirty monotonous job to another boring, dirty monotonous job. And somehow you're supposed to come out of it all 'enriched'. But I never feel 'enriched' — I just feel knackered.

> (Nichols and Beynon, 1977, p. 16.)

Conclusions

The first part of this chapter analyses the significance of Taylorism for job design and argues that its influence, though considerable, did not follow a simple pattern in British industrial history. Taylorism was essentially based on job fragmentation though it was often modified in its implementation and, as we have argued elsewhere, a mixture of labour strategies was possible (see Littler, 1982; Littler & Salaman, 1982).

Fordism was a distinct labour management strategy in that it was systemic, requiring the re-organisation of the entire factory, and involved non-Taylorite control techniques. But it also took over the basic job design dynamics of Taylorism. The internationalisation of technology and the mechanism of the multi-national corporation assisted the spread of both Taylorism and Fordism, especially in the mass production industries.

Taylorism and Fordism as forms of work organisation are constrained by certain economic and technical limits and carry coordination and control costs. In particular Taylorism and Fordism are set within a certain pattern of product markets and inter-capitalist competition. In the late 1960s and early 1970s it began to look as though the accumulation of labour problems plus the shift in product markets, necessitating greater flexibility and with an emphasis on quality and reliability, were creating a crisis for Fordism.

However, reorganised assembly lines and group technology remained limited experiments. In general, these new ideas of job design and work organisation had a very limited influence: they remained the gospel peddled by a few avant-garde consultants. But past history suggests that the succeeding decade (the 1980s in this case) may be the period of the widespread take-up of managerial innovations. Two inter-linked factors reinforce this potentiality — the continuing economic crisis of the 1980s plus the pressures of Japanese competition. The 1980s, like the 1930s, will no doubt spur some employers to cut wages (there have been several cases of this), extend work hours in some form, or impose straightforward labour intensification involving no attempt at work reorganisation. Clearly, mass unemployment has shifted economic power to the employers, so that they can force through previously unacceptable changes amidst a climate of fear and uncertainty about jobs. But there is a limit to what can be achieved by economic coercion. In particular it ignores the changing nature of competition. An emphasis on quality rather than the velocity of throughput means that reluctant acquiescence has to give way to active cooperation. Of course for some employers automation and robots appear to offer a solution — but not enough of one. The crisis of Fordism is neatly exemplified by the present dilemma of Ford Europe. Faced with the large productivity gap between its European plants and Japanese manufacturers, Ford set up its 'After Japan' programme, which as the headlines announced was a contradictory mix of robots, job cuts, a union struggle *and* an attempt to engage the enthusiasm and willingness of the workers (see *The Guardian*, 11 June 1980).

The present Ford (and Fordist) dilemma illustrates the essential tension in the capital/labour relationship — a tension between the need to regulate and dominate the production process versus the need to maximise the creativity and reliability of wage labour. This chapter has revolved around fundamental elements in the history of this contradiction.

6 · Technology and Work

Machines alone do not give us mass production. Mass production is achieved by both machines and men. And while we have gone a long way toward perfecting our mechanical operations, we have not successfully written into our equations whatever complex factors represent Man, the human element.

Henry Ford II.

This chapter will explore current developments in work design and work technology — particularly those developments which involve the extension of mechanisation and automation to the limits represented by robots and other forms of computer-based work systems. A major objective of the chapter is simply to describe and organise a complex and rapidly shifting picture. But another related objective is to locate these developments firmly within the framework of analysis argued earlier in the book. In chapter three we quoted from Mandel who argues that under conditions of competition, or of profit squeeze, a major strategy for capital is '...the intensification of automation, or in other words, the concentration of investment to set free as much living labour as possible...' (Mandel, 1978, p. 182.) Furthermore, Mandel, and numerous other commentators, note that a dominant tendency within the development of corporation structure and strategy is the ever more pervasive spread of control over all sources of uncertainty which can destabilise the corporation's long term planning and investment. A particularly important focus for such increasing control is over the level and intensity of workers' effort. Chapters 4 and 5 catalogue some of the options available to management and some of the contradictions that accompany them. Corporations can seek greater control over labour. But frequently such efforts result, ultimately, in a *reduction* in predictability. Chapter 5 plotted various corporate strategies which started from the premise that to achieve control you must first lose, or delegate control (or appear to...). But that chapter also showed that such efforts too soon stumble over their own contradictions: control can not be reallocated a piece at a time.

This chapter describes a new, and apparently even more tempting solution to the old and hitherto insoluble problem of management: to *eliminate* 'Man, the human element' completely. Such options, in so far as they are now technologically feasible, appear to present management with a radically new strategy. This chapter describes these developments and considers how far the use of robots, or computer-based work systems, actually solves capital's problems with labour, or simply transforms the nature of the problems.

Technology has a powerful influence on work processes and work organisation. This is not because of some technological determinism, but because of two inter-linked factors. First, the separation of execution and design, a separation measured both physically (with all the design and planning done in a separate department or organisation) and socially ('the engineer never speaks to us'), results in the externalisation of technology. Second, this separation has resulted in the emergence and diffusion of a technocratic ideology so that jobs and tasks and peoples' working lives are treated as the residual factor of the relationship between machines and products. The most striking thing about most British factories is that job design is *nobody's* responsibility. Certainly the typical line manager does not spend his day thinking about job design. So how do jobs get 'designed'? The common managerial view is outlined by L. E. Davis:

> ... there is still a strong commitment to the proposition that meeting the requirements of the technology (process, equipment) will yield superior job performance, measured by organisationally relevant criteria, and a deep-seated conviction that the same performance will not be achieved if technological requirements are not given exclusive consideration.

(Davis & Taylor, 1972, pp. 300-1).

It is this implicit orientation and priority that makes it conventional to conceptualise the 'impact of technological change'. But if we fracture this way of thinking, then it is possible to see that there are several stages of human choice involved. The configuration of choice itself varies. With the automation of process production, such as chemicals, involving large capital-intensive plants, technical change tends to take the form of complete new plants. When workers and operational management are introduced to the plant, decisions regarding the organisation of work are largely built-in and the area of choice is limited. With the automation of other types of production there has often been a process of incremental innovation, allowing a broader area of choice (Wilkinson, 1983).

However, even if machinery and equipment are designed and constructed by humans (rather than by the iron monster ruling the organisational realm dreamed up by theorists such as Ellul (1964)), it is not alterable by them *at will*. This is because of the development costs attached to any new pattern of work activity. Where the fragmentation of jobs around a new machine has occurred historically, then the costs of developing some alternative technology may be considerable. Moreover, the technical choice involving a Taylorite configuration of labour may result in a short-term productivity gain which could eliminate any competitors pursuing a longer-term strategy under market conditions (see C.S.S. Report, 1981, pp. 79-80).

Bearing in mind that technology has to be viewed in this broader social and economic context, then it is useful to make a distinction between the processes of mechanisation and automation before considering the nature and effects of factory and office automation in the rest of the chapter.

Generally the replacement of muscle power, both human and animal, by machine power is termed 'mechanisation'. This was the industrial and social transformation which we associate with the industrial revolution. In contrast, the replacement of human judgement, monitoring and control by machine process is termed 'automation'. These distinctions are not absolute, and some automation occurred in the nineteenth century. But the widespread availability of electronic devices after the 1950s, and their miniaturisation and cheapening during the 1970s with the advent of micro-processors, has certainly resulted in a qualitative shift towards more automatic production processes. The full implications of this transformation are still being lived through and in this chapter we can only consider the most important aspects.

'Robby' the robot

By now robots have become so familiar in some factories as to have received names — 'Robby' being the most common. Typically robots conform to the standard configuration of a jointed arm, bolted to the floor or perhaps to an overhead platform. The arm can rotate about a vertical axis, and at the end of the arm is a 'wrist' with two or three joints on which can be mounted a range of tools or grippers. The robot is powered by an electronic or hydraulic motor and is controlled by a minicomputer. Robots vary in size and load capacities: they may be capable of lifting only a few pounds or many tons. Also robots vary in their flexibility (mobile robots are still experimental) and in the accuracy with which they can position objects.

At present robots lack not only mobility but sensing devices. They are programmed by leading them through the tasks they have to perform. For example, in spot welding a worker who is familiar with the job will hold the spot welding gun in the robot's arm and go through the motion of welding the specific series of spots on the component. 'During this time the drive to the robot is disconnected, but it records the motions in its computer. When the drive is re-connected it will repeat exactly the operations carried out by the man, moving the gun at the same speed through the same path.' (C.S.S. Report, 1981, p. 60.) In such cases the transfer of manual skill from man to machine is overt and evident.

In general robots are doing welding, spray-painting, de-burring and similar tasks, but increasingly they are moving into wider areas of work. A West German study of 1,000 industrial jobs suggested that at present only 2% could be done by robots, but if an elementary sensing device were added then the proportion would shoot up to 35% (C.S.S. Report, 1981, p. 61). The future reality is that sensing robots are likely to be common in the 1990s (*New Scientist*, 6 Jan 1983; for a classification of present robot applications see Zermeno *et al.,* 1980, Table 4.1).

The car industry is one which is rapidly making use of robots. British Leyland's Metro line is well-known, but Ford had set up 120 robots on the Sierra line at Dagenham by 1982 and plan to introduce another 30. The Dagenham robots cope with a variety of tasks, welding, handling materials and sealing. Nearly 90% of the Sierra's welds are done by robots. But despite the Metro and Dagenham lines, the British car industry has been slow to invest in robotics. In West Germany the major car companies have invested heavily in the new technology. For example, Volkswagen has already installed 650 robots at its Wolfsburg plant and plans to have 2,000 there before 1990. Many of the existing Japanese car plants demonstrate the potential of robot lines: for example the Mazda plant at Togo Kogyo is capable of putting together a front-wheel drive small hatchback, a rear-drive medium saloon and a rotary-engined sports car *on the same production line in succession.* The significance of this is that instead of closing down the factory and re-tooling for a new model every few years, the production line can be re-programmed to make new car models with undreamt-of flexibility (*The Financial Times,* 19 Oct 1982).

Robots are being used, or experimented with, in many industries, apart from their much publicised use in car plants. Rowntree Mackintosh has investigated buying 160 robots to put chocolates into boxes (a traditionally labour-intensive task), Wallop Industries employs robots to pack boxes of high explosives because of the dangerous nature of the task, whilst Lyle and Scott are experimenting with robots to act as indirect 'workers' transferring materials between sewing machines in the clothing industry. Ultimately, in the latter case, the objective is to link robots with automatic sewing machines which could stitch garments together under computer control without the intervention of human operators (*New Scientist,* 27 March 1980, 19 Feb 1981, 18 Feb 1982). This last application of robots is particularly interesting as part of the struggle by the British textile and clothing industry to cope with the surge of imports from low cost countries.

However, although the robots are coming (125,000 in the world in 1982; 1,000 in Britain), they are not coming that fast. A study by Fleck showed that of 32 cases of robot adoption in the UK, 44% were initial failures and in half of these cases the use of robots was abandoned (Fleck, 1983). Successful development of a robot installation can take two years, because the robot needs to be linked to input and output feeders and to the overall production process. Moreover, because of lack of trained maintenance staff, many robots can be seen 'on strike' on factory floors waiting for electronic technicians to come from overseas. Robots are far from being infallible: Japanese figures show that three out of four break down before completing 1,500 hours work, whilst nearly one in three experience problems before 100 hours (*New Scientist,* 6 Jan 1983).

Despite the development problems, the long-term potential employment effects of robots are dramatic. The evidence so far is that robots produce about 30% more than a human worker, but they can work all day so that each robot displaces about two and half people (Fleck 1983; similar figures are given by Japanese employers, for example see Ikuro Takagi, 1982, p. 18). But apart from creating unemployment, what effects, if any, have robots had on job design and skill levels? The evidence is still scanty. In Japan, where the use of robots has been the most extensive (70% of the estimated world population of robots), they have been mainly used to fill a gap occasioned by a serious shortage of skilled welders. In Britain robots have been used on dirty or hazardous work and, surprisingly perhaps, in *low-pay* industries. British trade unions have usually agreed to the installation of robots in these circumstances provided workers have been found other jobs. In other words robots have been taking over restricted, dirty, fragmented jobs which few people want to cling to anyway. Thus, there are few direct skill effects. Fleck's work has suggested that there has been some slight increase in job monotony, especially where an operator instead of working, say, an injection moulding machine to his own rhythm, now simply services a robot who works two or three machines. The overall sense of machine pacing intensifies. This is certainly the case on flow lines where workers are faced with robots at adjacent work stations.

A different organisation of work could prevent an intensification of job monotony. It is possible to combine programming and setting functions with the remaining monotonous tasks, creating a new type of job. But such a step would require considerable training and cut across the process of labour cheapening, and there is no sign of this type of development (Zermeno *et al.,* 1980, p. 195).

The unmanned factory

Robots grab media attention because unlike most machines they resemble human beings and because they have an aura of science fiction about them, but so far their development has been piecemeal, especially in Britain, where the pattern is one of a *few* robots in *many* firms. Perhaps the more significant development is the potential, or promise, of the wholly automated unmanned factory.

As has been suggested in the previous section, robots so far have been largely employed on fairly basic tasks that many workers find unpleasant, such as paint spraying. The next step is to integrate many robots or automated machines into unmanned assembly lines. Assembly robots are technically possible but as yet they do not make economic sense, particularly in a low-wage country like Britain. Moreover, even in high-wage economies like Japan, there are employer fears about the mass replacement of assembly-line workers by robots (*The Financial Times,* 21 Oct 1981). However, as the use of various forms of robots spreads so their cost (£20,000–£50,000) will be much lower and the pay-off in increased profit will override employer caution.

The barriers, then, to the unmanned mass production factory are economic, political and social. The barriers to the unmanned batch production factory so far have been technological.

As was pointed out in Chapter 5, hitherto only a small proportion of industrial goods have been made with traditional automation. Most metal goods are made in small batches of a few hundreds at a time for which automation would be too expensive. Ford-type production requires specialised machinery which is highly inflexible. Automated specialised machinery is even more expensive and inflexible and only manufacturers producing items in thousands or millions can afford large scale investment in it. But recently, following a revolution in technology, the principle of automation has begun to spread beyond the confines of mass production to batch production systems.

The technology is called 'flexible manufacturing systems' (FMS) and consists of three basic elements: a set of machinery stations, a transfer mechanism, and a central computer which oversees the whole operation. The principles of an FMS are best seen in an example. One of the most famous automated factories is the Yamazaki machine tool plant in Japan. The factory consists of 18 flexible machining centres which can perform a variety of metal-shaping/cutting operations, plus a variety of other automatic machines. The transfer of work from machine to machine is automatically regulated by computer. In most engineering plants it is necessary to replace the machine tools (that is the cutting and shaping blades) on a regular basis. In the Yamazaki plant all the tools are mounted on a travelling drum stand and are automatically replaced; wear is measured with an automatic measuring device. The entire operation of the factory, including accounts, the preparation of financial statements, and production control, is performed automatically. The factory reception area contains a flashing number board which gives the latest production total: it changes every 45 minutes, the average time it takes to complete a Mazak machine tool. The factory has three shifts – the first shift employs seven people, the second five, and the night shift runs without anybody (*The Financial Times*, 21 Oct 1981).

What are the likely effect of FMSs in the future? They will still need people, though as we can see from the Japanese example, not many. There are the unskilled tasks of loading and unloading parts, and of cleaning and clearing the equipment. Second, there will be the semi-skilled tasks of changing tools where automatic changing is too difficult, at least for the present. Third, there are the skilled electrician and programmer jobs – necessay in case the system goes haywire. But overall the employment impact is likely to be immense. A four-station FMS could be run by two or three people and do the work of a small factory containing 50 or more people equipped with *advanced* numerically controlled machines, let alone a traditional plant employing twice as many.

This impact will not be felt overnight. There are still less than 100 FMSs in the world, half of them in Japan. And most of these plants are not totally 'flexible'. They can turn out a variety of products by re-programming the computer, but only within the same 'family' of items. For example, they can make a range of tubes or casings, but *not* a mixture of both kinds of product. Britain, admittedly ten years behind, only opened its first FMS plant in 1982, and it will take further advances in technique before unmanned factories are a commonplace reality. Some observers consider the unmanned factory an exception – an extreme case which will never be typical. Certainly there is a huge gulf between a highly automated plant staffed by a group of monitors and machine tenders and the factory with no-one on the shop-floor. The reality in the immediate future probably lies somewhere in between, but even this reality implies massive changes in work and working practices. Factories will be smaller (FMS requires 40% less floor space), more flexible, and able to react faster to changes in demand, so that stocks can be kept low. Most crucially from our point of view, the labour content of the production process will be drastically reduced, perhaps cheapening engineering goods, but shunting many millions into dole queues.

The impact of automated batch production on jobs and skills is still indeterminate. At present we seem to be in a phase of development where the 'new' technology is genuinely new, that is, it appears to be malleable and to offer a range of options – centralisation versus decentralisation; enhancement of skills versus polarisation of skills away from the shop floor; rigid job control versus delegation of decision-making over production. As yet the options have not been closed off by a series of decisions and technical developments which in combination result in an irrevocable situation. We return to this general question in the conclusions of Chapter 6. The next section considers the impact of information technology on office work.

Information technology and the revolution in the office

The raw material of office work is information. People and machines in offices generate new information, collect information from outside, store, copy, process, transmit and present it in a variety of ways. But office work has often been marked by high costs and low productivity. The classic indicator of this is the personal secretary as a status symbol, given that few managers generate sufficient work to keep a secretary busy for eight hours per day. In 1917 Leffingwell advocated the application of Taylor's principles to office work and in 1925 he attacked what he called the 'private secretary evil'. But in general these attacks on the 'social office' had little effect (see Leffingwell, 1917 and 1925; Braverman, 1974, pp. 305-12; Downing 1980, pp. 278-9).

Two factors have inhibited the rationalisation of office work. Firstly, there have been the social factors alluded to above. Such work, though occurring within a bureaucratic framework in large-scale organisations, has still depended on personal interaction, gossip in the corridor, and informal methods of control. This has been particularly true of male/female office relationships since women were brought in as office labour in the latter part of the nineteenth century, following the spread of literacy. Secondly, the technical means by which office work could be completely reorganised have been lacking until the 1970s.

The key to change was the technical ability to convert all information, including words and text, into a digital form so that it could be understood by a computer. In any computer, information is stored and processed in the form of a chain of 0's and 1's — binary digits called 'bits'. For example, a typical A4 page in computer code has about 10,000 bits. The capacity to convert all the raw material of an office into computer code opens up the possibility of transforming office work by bringing together a number of different technologies — this is the so-called information revolution. But the initial manifestations of the new technology will be developments from existing products and techniques. Therefore we will focus on a well understood machine, the typewriter, and a familiar job, that of the typist, to see how information technology may affect them.

Automatic typewriters with a memory first appeared about fifty years ago, but the technology did not become reliable and sufficiently cheap until the 1960s. These machines permitted a typist to make limited corrections, (i.e. to 'edit'), by re-playing the memory and making alterations to the text at appropriate points. The machines could be used to reproduce standard letters, with the typist filling in variable information such as names, addresses and dates.

The next stage in the 1970s was the addition of a minicomputer, giving the machine an enhanced memory and a processing capacity, plus a screen (a visual display unit, or 'VDU') enabling the text to be visually displayed for editing. This package is, of course, known as a word-processor. The output of the machine, the printer (which may be a separate machine), only prints, at speeds of up to 2,000 lines per minute, when the text has been satisfactorily edited.

Word processors are still not cheap (£4,000-£5,000) and this has inhibited their diffusion. Figures on the diffusion and use of word processors are not readily available, but some indication is provided by the following table for the USA and Western Europe:

Table 1 *Sales value of word processors in USA and Western Europe, 1977-79* ($ m.)

	1977	1978	% increase	1979	% increase
USA	800	1,000	25%	1,200	20%
W. Europe	144	186	29%	243	30%

1979 figures are estimates, and all figures are rounded.

Source: *Electronics,* 4 Jan 1979

Table 1 shows that whatever the price barriers, the installation of word processors was proceeding at a rapid pace in the late seventies. But what does the take up of this new technology mean for the traditional role of the typist? Typically the technology is being implemented with the following features:

1. Relations between bosses and secretaries are tending to become depersonalised and word processing centres are being set up to offer a general typing service. Such a system is no different in essence from the old typing pool, except that the costs of the capital equipment now mean that most firms are forced to establish such centres.

2. Most of the new word processors require minimum operator training and with shared print-out facilities the operator may not even *see* what she has keyboarded, because the printer may be housed in a separate room.

3. Word processors permit for the first time the accurate measurement of typists' output and productivity — automatically. Thus it is possible to establish managerial control systems linking bonuses and other benefits (e.g. extra holiday entitlements) to operators' productivities (cf. Braverman, 1974, pp. 333-4).

4. As the use of word processors increases, most typists will cease to think of themselves, however vaguely, as potential or even actual secretaries and become keyboard operators, their task range narrowed down to one continuous, tightly monitored and controlled function. This in turn will set up a polarisation between top secretarial, quasi-administrative jobs on the one hand and the mass of women keyboard operators. Moreover this polarisation is likely to reflect and reinforce class divisions. In the nineteenth century many working class women went into service, becoming servants in large and not-so-large households: a job which gave many of them acquaintance with middle and upper-class life styles. In the twentieth century office work became the respectable occupation for working-class as well as middle-class women and office service replaced household service, However, as we have suggested, one effect of the new office technology is to create a mass of lower-level office jobs occupied by working-class women operating under the pressures of traditional factory labour. Not even the most fantasy-prone mind will be able to pretend that there is an element of social mobility involved.

5. The introduction of word-processors and expensive associated equipment is likely to result in a change in office hours, at least in large bureaucratic organisations. Because of pressure by management to obtain the maximum utilisation of the equipment and reduce the pay-back period, there is a tendency towards the introduction of shift-work. This is now common in the USA, and there are some signs of a 'twilight shift' (6 p.m. to 10 p.m.) in large British organisations. An added incentive for such hours of work is that the post office lines, which can transmit typed copy from one word processor to another, are cheaper to use in the evenings (Downing *et al.,* 1978, App., p. 3).

Overall, the early effects of new technology in the office seem to be a tendency to establish formal methods of control over de-personalised workers in a classical Taylorite manner. This seems ironic when the struggles on the factory floor have led to at least a verbal modification of Taylorite and Fordist principles of job design in industrial work areas.

The employment effects of automated offices could, like automated factories, be dramatic. Typically, consultancy firms and equipment manufacturers claim that word processors can do the work of 2½ to 5 traditional typists. Similarly, there have been suggestions that 40% of typists' jobs could disappear (Downing *et al.,* 1978, App., pp. 1-2). Barron and Curnow (1979) estimated that there were one million typists and secretaries in Britain plus a further 750,000 office workers in administration and 400,000 in management. Thus the disappearance of 40% of routine office jobs could mean the loss of between 400,000 and 700,000 jobs. However, much of this is still speculation. To date, productivity gains in offices have been small, if indeed there have been any at all (*The Financial Times,* 2 Mar 1981), and detailed figures on job losses are not available.

The technical possibilities of office automation are well mapped out – every manager to be equipped with a keyboard, VDU, minicomputer and communicating word processors. Typists would go the way of scriveners. But at present the prices of much equipment are not low enough for widespread introduction to be practical, though Britain is not typical. Automation is lagging behind in the UK and is more evident on the office floors of the USA and West Germany.

Apart from the question of price, there is the widespread social resistance mentioned above. Most managers have shown a marked resistance to using a keyboard. Even in the USA, where many managers are taught to type, there is still such resistance because typing is considered demeaning. This reflects the managerial desire to preserve the customary structures of manager/ subordinate and manager/secretary. It may yet turn out to be the case that managerial resistance to office automation prevents the worst consequences of the office revolution in terms of both employment and de-personalised work.

There has certainly been considerable trade union disquiet about the new office technology. Throughout the world trade unions have criticised many features of it on the grounds that it damages the working environment. This has resulted in the establishment of national standards in Scandinavia and West Germany. In Britain white-collar unions, such as ASTMS and APEX, have produced guidelines on standards for equipment. But worker resistance is muted by the nature of the white-collar labour market: there is a high turnover of office staff plus a widescale use of temporary workers and part-timers, all of which makes long-term union organisation difficult to achieve.

Thus, managerial resistance as much as clerical worker opposition has forced some rethinking of the new technology by equipment manufacturers. There has been some shift from mechanistic models of work, focusing on information flow and the processing of data, to humanistic models which take more account of the activities of the workers involved (see *New Scientist*, 5 Nov 1981). But here we return to the question of technological choice. Word processors and associated equipment, based as closely as possible on traditional ways of working in the office, are expensive, so that employers are faced with a choice between an expensive system that will produce less disturbance to established office procedures and relationships, and a cheaper system that will require extensive reorganisation and may incur strong resistance.

Conclusions

Three general themes are raised by this overview of factory and office automation. Firstly, we have emphasised that there is no technological determinism. The specification and adoption of new technology is subject to human choice — a process which is shaped by conflicts and struggles between different groups. Though the conflict between labour and capital is fundamental, in each case this pattern is complicated by divisions within management as well as between workers.

After the 'microprocessor revolution' hit the headlines in the 1970s, the TUC responded to the potential threats to employment and work routines by advocating collective bargaining specifically over the new technology. The aim of these so-called New Technology Agreements (NTAs) was that trade unions and workers should be involved in the specification and selection of new equipment. Though a significant advance on the traditional neglect of job content, the influence extended by bargainers so far has proved minimal. Partly this is the result of the weakening of trade union bargaining power during the economic depression, with the continuing haemorrhage of union members and funds. Partly too it is the result of lack of expertise on the union side; shop-floor representatives become the passive consumers of detailed technical information made available at consultation or participation committees (Winch, 1982). But partly also it is due to the fact that proposed technological change hits people unevenly. Some workers face redundancy, others are offered more secure but more routinised jobs, yet other groups are offered enhanced status associated with new technical toys. Moreover, some of the areas affected most by new technology, lower-grade office work and the retail sector for example, are staffed by very vulnerable groups of workers with no tradition of workplace bargaining or resistance.

In general, trade unionists and workers as members of employing organisations feel themselves facing an insoluble dilemma on jobs. If the new technology is introduced, then jobs will disappear, but if automation is ignored jobs will disappear anyway as market position is eroded by more innovative competitors.

The second general argument arising from the debate over technology and work is that between pessimistic and optimistic views of the future. The pessimistic view, associated with writers like Braverman, emphasises that the employer's search for economic and technical efficiency within the capitalist framework of intense competition results in labour rationalisation, mass redundancy, and the restructuring of work towards more fragmented, routinised tasks (Braverman, 1974; Zimbalist, 1979). The optimistic view underlines that technological innovation results in more and better trained workers exercising increased autonomy in their jobs whilst the more arduous and repetitive tasks are assigned to machines. As the Japanese Robot Industry Association says, robots are 'tools for the liberation of mankind' creating enhanced leisure for all (Littler, 1982, pp. 12-13; *New Scientist,* 6 Jan 1983).

The evidence so far does not encourage us to take the optimistic view. However, one complicating factor in assessing the two viewpoints is that of the probable time scale. For the development of new technologies in both factory and office this is difficult to estimate, even if the general directions of change are discernible. Look at the following prediction: 'During the next few years, we shall probably see more and more robots, so that ultimately business and factories will be run by only a small proportion of the people now employed.' (Golding.) That statement was made not in 1983, but *fifty* years ago in 1933! Similarly, the debate over the effects of automation in the 1950s and 1960s parallels much of the present-day debate about new technology. But common to the prophets of both boom and gloom was a contraction of the time scale. In the event, the expected effects of the introduction of computers and data processing did not immediately materialise and their application was largely concentrated in specific industrial sectors (Marsh, 1981; C.S.S. Report, 1981, pp. 69-70). Similarly we may now be overestimating the pace of change, and the pressing consequences of the new technology may be a problem for our sons and daughters in a restructured labour market. Maybe, but two factors suggest not: the depth and persistence of the capitalist recession and the accelerated forces of competition.

We cannot take recent British industrial history as a guide, because increasingly over the past thirty years British industry has been lagging behind other economies in its take-up and implementation of automation and new techniques. In addition, the severity of the present recession is creating an increasing urgency for major Western organisations to cut costs and restore profit levels. The 1980s parallel should not be the expansionary decades of the 1950s and 1960s, but the 1930s. The latter decade was the period when the forces of economic depression made it imperative that firms reduce labour and capital costs in order to survive. Taylorite methods of labour rationalisation were widely diffused during that period. In the context of the new depression it is the diffusion of robotics and office automation which appears to offer an avenue of survival for many employers, not only against high cost competitors in developed economies but even against low cost competitors in the Pacific Basin and elsewhere. Thus General Motors, which has already laid off thousands of American car workers, plans to introduce 14,000 robots in its American plants by 1990, primarily as a response to the Japanese threat. Clearly the employment effects of the new technology will be much greater during a persistent recession than during a period (such as the 1950s and 1960s) when demand for goods was rising.

The third general problem area relates to the fact that we cannot consider the quantity of employment without considering its quality: the two are intertwined. Both unemployment and dead-end machine feeding represent wastes of human ability. This raises the question of the relation between skill and the new technology, a question which returns us to Taylorism – a topic considered in Chapter 5.

Taylorism helped to generate a view of industrial and technical knowledge which counterposed science and traditional human judgement: the latter was viewed as rule of thumb inefficiency. In essence Taylorism offered a 'mechanisation of knowledge', in which implicit knowledge has no place. The ideal is envisaged as a sequential application of explicit techniques which squeezes out human skill 'as an essentially bounded embodiment of what was known inexactly and pragmatically in the past' (C.S.S. Report 1981, p. 74).

Opposed to the Taylorite view of science is what we can call the 'tool view', as exemplified by the job of the aircraft pilot. A modern pilot sits atop a machine of ever increasing power and complexity which he must learn to master. At times the plane can be turned over to automatic, but the on-board computers are tools and he is free to reject their conclusions when he considers it necessary to do so.

At present, modern technology seems to incorporate Taylorite conceptions of human skills, both factory and office automation having a tendency to create fragmented tasks with restructured or non-existent areas of task discretion. Moreover, as we pass through a rapid period of technical change many choices will have to be made; if they all follow the same Taylorite mode, the costs of choosing an alternative technology will become higher and higher and reversal of the process impossible.

7 · Class and the Labour Process

Recent theories of class

This book has outlined the continued reality of work-based inequalities in relation to pay, conditions, job security and health. However, as we pointed out, this is only one aspect of class at work. More fundamental are the inequalities of power: the day-to-day experience of this type of inequality is vividly caught by Wright Mills (1951):

> Seen from below, the management is not a Who but a series of Theys and even Its. Management is something one reports to in some office, maybe in all offices including that of the union; it is a printed instruction and a sign on a bulletin board; it is the voice coming through the loudspeakers; it is the name in the newspaper; it is the signature you can never make out, except it is printed underneath; it is a system that issues orders superior to anybody you know close-up; it blueprints, specifying in detail, your work-life and the boss-life of your foreman. Management is the centralized say-so.
>
> Seen from the middle ranks, management is one-part people who give you the nod, one-part system, one-part yourself. White-collar people may be part of management, like they say, but management is a lot of things, not all of them managing. You carry authority, but you are not its source. As one of the managed, you are on view from above, and perhaps you are seen as a threat; as one of the managers, you are seen from below, perhaps as a tool. You are the cog and the beltline of the bureaucratic machinery itself; you are a link in the chains of commands, persuasions, notices, bills, which bind together the men who make decisions and the men who make things, without you the managerial demiurge could not be. But your authority is confined strictly within a prescribed orbit of occupational actions, and such power as you wield is a borrowed thing. Yours is the sub-ordinate's mark, yours the canned talk. The money you handle is somebody else's money; the papers you sort and shuffle already bear somebody else's marks. You are the servant of decision, the assistant of authority, the minion of management. You are closer to management than the wage-workers are, but yours is seldom the last decision.
>
> Seen from close to the top, management is the ethos of the higher circle: concentrate power, but enlarge your staff. Down the line, make

them feel a part of what you are a part. Set up a school for managers and manage what managers learn, open a channel of two-way communication: commands go down, information comes up. Keep a firm grip but don't boss them, boss their experience; don't let them learn what you don't tell them. Between decision and execution, between command and obedience, let there be reflex. Be calm, judicious, rational; groom your personality and control your appearance; make business a profession. Develop yourself. Write a memo; hold a conference with men like you. And in all this be yourself and be human: nod gravely to the girls in the office; say hello to the men; and always listen carefully to the ones above: 'Over last week end, I gave much thought to the information you kindly tendered me on Friday, especially...'

(Mills, 1951, pp. 80-81)

By examining power in the workplace, Wright Mills arrives at a conventional three-class model, in opposition to the simple Marxian model of capital and wage labour. Other observers, especially those who have worked on the shop-floor, have underlined the difficulties of translating an abstract theory of class to the realities of the workshop:

There was no common experience of working on the shop floor. Workers in different grades were separated by their specialisms, place in the hierarchy, and particular pay and conditions. Operators did only manual work tied to the line, while the chargehands' and supervisors' administrative responsibilities involved walking around to oversee the work. The engineers' tasks were technical, and more high-powered. Looking at the hierarchy from the position of a woman operator, there was a very basic divide between those who ran the line and those who were run by it — the engineers and supervisors on one side, and us on the other. We did the hardest work and got the worst deal.

(Cavendish, 1982, p. 166)

We can see in this example of work in a motor components factory that the division of labour and relative dependence 'on the line' overrode broad class identifications.

These repeated difficulties about class categories have led to theoretical critiques of Marxian class theory. There have been four general criticisms:

1 Society does not consist of two monolithic groups. Instead there are numerous competing groups, formed around various axes. Therefore, a multi-factor model of class and society is necessary.

2 In general, the apparent simplicity of the Marxian model disguises the fact that it is difficult to draw the boundary lines between classes. There are many grey areas, and no agreement about how to categorise many wage-earners, such as supervisors, technicians, etc. (Wright, 1976, p. 3.)

3 Is an economic criterion adequate? Should a new class map be based on political and ideological criteria as well?

4 Are Marxian class categories action groups? Is there a one-to-one correspondence between relations to the means of production and relations in the political sphere? Is the relation of the individual to property a crucial determinant of social action?

These criticisms have given rise to two recent attempts to draw new class maps of capitalist societies — namely the work of Poulantzas and that of Erik Olin Wright.

Poulantzas in his book *Classes in Contemporary Capitalism* (1975), was concerned to combat 'economism'. He insisted that class relations cannot be understood solely in terms of economic relations, and consequently, attempted to integrate political and ideological factors into a class analysis. In essence, Poulantzas's analysis used three distinctions:

1 At the economic level, the distinction between productive and unproductive labour is used to draw the boundary around the working class. This criterion results in a very restricted definition of the working class.

2 At the political level, the basic distinction is between authority and non-authority positions. Poulantzas argues that the work of management and supervisors reproduces within the production process itself the political relations of domination between the capitalist class and the working class.

3 Ideological domination is based on the division of labour between mental and manual work. The notions of expertise and technocracy help to legitimate employer authority and reproduce the relations of domination.

Poulantzas uses these general criteria to construct four classes — the bourgeoisie, the proletariat, the old petty bourgeoisie and the *new* petty bourgeoisie. As can be seen, the new class which emerges is the 'new petty bourgeoisie', consisting of white-collar employees, technicians, supervisors, etc. This class, claims Poulantzas, is ideologically and politically similar to the position of the old petty bourgeoisie.

The main, detailed criticism of Poulantzas has been put forward by Wright. This consists of several points. Firstly, the distinction between productive and unproductive labour is misconceived. Many jobs contain both productive and unproductive elements. In general, 'most labour in capitalist society has both productive and unproductive aspects. The productive/unproductive labour distinction should thus be thought of as reflecting two dimensions of labour activity, rather than two types of wage-earners.' (Wright, 1976, p. 16). Moreover, there is little reason to suppose that productive and unproductive social positions have different class interests. Secondly, Poulantzas's political criterion for defining class positions stretches the meaning of 'political' beyond acceptable limits. In essence he is concerned with positions in the supervisory hierarchy, which is not a political aspect of relationships in a conventional sense. Thirdly, Poulantzas's use of the mental/manual division appears arbitrary. Whilst the mental/manual division creates divisions within classes, it does not, any more than sexual divisions, 'constitute criteria for class boundaries in its own right.' (Wright, 1976, p. 20; contrast Wright, 1980, p. 10). Fourthly, the new petty bourgeoisie seems a residual, heterogeneous category, partly created by Poulantzas's very narrow conception of the working class. Certainly it is a grouping which is not defined in terms of consistent economic criteria (Nichols, 1981, p. 34). Even if Poulantzas's rejection of economism is granted, then he accords priority to the economic, the political and the ideological in an arbitrary and inconsistent way.

Wright himself puts forward a novel theorisation of class. The starting point is that capitalist class relations are the congealed outcome of several historical transformations. Therefore, if the major structural changes in the course of capitalist development are delineated, this provides a grounded set of criteria for defining class positions. Wright suggests that there have been three central processes: 'the progressive loss of control over the labour process on the part of the direct producers; the elaboration of complex authority hierarchies within capitalist enterprises and bureaucracies; and the differentiation of various functions originally embodied in the entrepreneurial capitalist.' (Wright, 1976, p. 28.)

The three historical developments described lead to the postulation of three processes or dimensions underlying the basic capital/labour relationship. These are:

1 Social relations of control over financial capital; i.e. control over the flow of investments and the capital accumulation process. This is equivalent to what Poulantzas called economic ownership.

2 Social relations of control over physical capital; i.e. control over the use and disposal of the non-human means of production.

3 Social relations of control over labour; i.e. control over supervision, discipline and training (see Wright, 1980, pp. 2-3).

At this point it should be noted that societies are not just modes of production. A society is always a particular, historical configuration involving more than a single mode of production. Thus most industrial societies involve social positions located within the capitalist mode of production, and within 'simple commodity production'; that is, within a system based on the production of commodities for the market by direct producers who employ no wage-labourers. Given this social formation, there are, according to Wright, three unambiguous class positions – the polarised capitalist and working classes plus the petty bourgeoisie – within the simple commodity mode of production (Wright, 1976, pp. 30-31).

The next step taken by Wright is to relax the assumption made by Poulantzas that class positions are all or nothing. Thus he arrives at the notion of *objectively contradictory class locations*, which are defined as positions in the class structure which are simultaneously in more than one class by reference to the three underlying dimensions which comprise class relations. There are two different types of contradictory location: firstly within the capitalist mode of production, and secondly between two modes of production. The assumptions lead to the following picture:

Figure 1   *The basic class relations of capitalist societies*

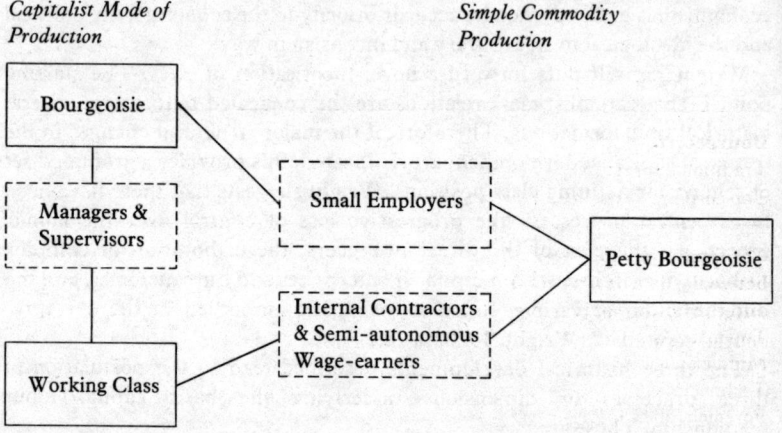

(Source: Based on Wright, 1980, Fig 1.1, p. 3. The dotted lines indicate contradictory class locations.)

Wright also emphasises that there are *levels* of control; in other words that the scope of control attached to organisational positions varies. This has partly arisen from the concentration of capital and the development of complex hierarchies, and partly this was always the case, even in the earliest enterprises. Wright distinguishes four levels of control in relation to his three dimensions: full, partial and minimal control, and a total lack of control.

The overall outcome of Wright's three inter-dependent dimensions of social class, plus the assumption of contradictory class relations, plus the assumption of four levels of control, is Table 1 which constitutes a new class map.

One further point in Wright's analysis needs to be underlined. Wright suggests that his conception of contradictory class locations provides a key to understanding the relevance of political and ideological factors whilst maintaining the primacy of economic relations. In essence his argument is that 'the extent to which political and ideological relations enter into the determination of class position is itself determined by the degree to which those positions occupy a contradictory location at the level of social relations of production' (Wright, 1976, pp. 39-40). In other words, it is the indeterminacy of class determinations at the economic level which allows

Table 1 *General criteria for class in Wright's analysis*

Social processes comprising class relations

	Economic Ownership	Relations of Possession	
	Control over investments, resources	Control over the physical means of production	Control over the labour power of others
Bourgeoisie			
Traditional capitalist	+	+	+
Top corporate executive	+	+	+
Contradictory location between the working class and the bourgeoisie			
Top managers	Partial/Minimal	+	+
Middle managers	Minimal/—	Partial	Partial
Technocrats	—	Minimal	Minimal
Foremen/line supervisors	—	—	Minimal
Working class	—	—	—
Contradictory location between the working class and the petty bourgeoisie			
Internal Contractors	Minimal/—	Partial	Partial
Semi-autonomous employees	—	Minimal	—
Petty bourgeoisie	+	+	—
Contradictory location between the petty bourgeoisie and the bourgeoisie			
Small employers	+	+	Minimal

(Source: Based on Wright, 1976, Chart 7, p. 33.)

political and ideological factors to become effective determinants of class attitudes and locations.

Wright's work represents an important advance on earlier class analysis, but apart from specific conceptual problems (see Nichols, 1981), the schema fails to grapple with some fundamental problems. Firstly, as Ehrenreich & Ehrenreich (1979) point out, the working class occupies, in this analysis, a *determinate* class location in which its class interest is fixed by its relation to the means of production. However, much recent labour process writing (e.g. Edwards, 1979) suggests that the working class is *not* constituted as a unified class confronting capital by the process of production. At any one point, the 'working class' is a collection of a number of perhaps highly-specific capital/wage labour relationships. The working class has no essence: 'In the normal circumstances of capitalist society, class is reflected in a much more fragmentary and uneven way.' (Thompson, 1983, p. 236.)

Apart from the continued over-determinate nature of Wright's class theory, there is the problem that it is a 'class map'. Though the theory is historically based, in that the three aspects of the social relations of production used to define class locations are founded on historical developments rather than *a priori* reasoning, nevertheless it is still too *static*. From our point of view, we want to know the relations between the dynamics of change in the labour process and the material basis for class formation.

Dynamics of the labour process and class formation

The recent work of Gordon, Edwards and Reich (1982) attempts to answer this question. They develop a conceptual framework which focuses on the sphere of production and links this to phases in the process of capital accumulation. Fundamental to their approach is the concept of 'social structures of accumulation'; this comprises the structure of the labour market and the system of labour management and control. The authors argue that the history of capitalism (at least in the United States) can be usefully divided into three clear, but overlapping, periods; the period of initial proletarianisation from the 1820s to the 1890s; the period of homogenisation of the working class from the 1890s to the Second World War; and the period of segmentation from the 1920s to the present (see Table 2). Thus, as is implied above, each of the three periods of capitalism is characterised by a different form of the labour process and different labour market structures.

Gordon *et al.* go further, and attempt to link changes in the labour process with macro-economic trends. During the period covered by Table 2, the 1790s to the 1970s, it is suggested that the world capitalist economy has been characterised by four successive long cycles of accumulation. These long swings, lasting for about fifty years, consist of a period of rapid growth and relatively high rates of profit (phase A in Table 2), and a succeeding period of stagnation and economic crisis (phase B). As can be seen from Table 2, a period of stagnation and crisis is associated with a stage of exploration, a lengthy period of research, experimentation and trial as employers search for a set of institutions which provide a stable and favourable context within which profits can be generated in production and realised through

Table 2 *Long swings and phases of the labour process in the United States*

Long Swings and Phases of Accumulation	Approximate Timing	Initial Proletarianisation	Homogenisation	Segmentation
IA	1790s to ca. 1820			
B	Ca. 1820 to Mid. 1840s	Exploration		
IIA	Mid. 1840s to ca. 1873	Consolidation		
B	Ca. 1873 to late 1890s	Decay	Exploration	
IIIA	Late 1890s to World War I		Consolidation	
B	World War I to World War II		Decay	Exploration
IVA	World War II to early 1970s			Consolidation
B	Early 1970s to present			Decay

Source: Gordon, Edwards and Reich, 1982, p. 12.

Note: Phase A is a period of rapid expansion and high profit rates.
Phase B is a period of economic stagnation and crisis.

exchange. A stage of exploration is followed by a stage of consolidation, when a new social structure of accumulation has been established resulting in a period of rapid accumulation. Such a period is brought to an end when the opportunities for profitable investment are blocked, choked off by cumulative impediments. These impediments are not exogenous factors which interfere with the accumulation process, but are generated by the accumulation process *itself*. When this period of decay occurs, capitalists do not have the choice of passively accepting the barriers to accumulation; instead a process of institutional reconstruction is set in motion, entailing a radical transformation of the organisation of work and a corresponding change in the structure of the labour market. Thus, a stage of decay and crisis is simultaneously a stage of exploration for the succeeding period.

According to Gordon *et al.*, employers, in their efforts to increase the efficiency of labour, impose workplace production patterns that shape the composition of the working class. During the initial proletarianisation phase, the expansion of capital depends on the establishment and legal enforcement of a system of private property ownership and the separation of peasants, small farmers, artisans, and so on from the means of production and the means of subsistence. The early period of exploration is the period of 'peasant workers', who typically have no pride of accomplishment in factory work and who, during business downturns, return to their original occupations and survive by working extremely hard under subsistence conditions (Sabel, 1982, pp. 101-9). An example would be the unskilled workers in Japan, known as 'dekasegi' workers, who floated back and forth between farm and factory (Littler, 1982, p. 148). Proletarianisation is complete and 'consolidated' when peasant workers give up the idea of themselves as temporary workers, a qualitative change which may have to await the succession of generations.

The composition of the working class, it is suggested, changed qualitatively around 1900, when there was 'a variety of direct and increasingly self-conscious corporate policies to reinforce the homogenisa-tion of labor' (Gordon *et al.,* 1982, p. 136). The overall pattern was the destruction of craft trade unions and a craft ethos, resulting in a mass of semi-skilled workers subject to a system of industrial authoritarianism, the 'drive system' (ibid., pp. 128-35).

Whereas Gordon *et al.*'s discussion of proletarianisation is relatively unproblematic, their discussion and dating of homogenisation is riven with difficulties. Essentially, they shift from the experience of a limited number of mass production industries in the USA to a general statement about *all* industries, ignoring the differences between them; ignoring the varieties of employer strategies and measures to control and incorporate labour; and ignoring the well-documented emergence of internal labour markets and labour segmentation which took place much earlier than they suggest (see Littler, 1983, pp. 189-90). As Nolan & Edwards (1982) point out, in an excellent critique, Gordon *et al.* substitute homogenisation and the drive system for Braverman's stress on Taylorism and deskilling which carries with it identical problems — the identification of one, single trend and 'the implication that it was universal and all-important' (ibid., p. 17).

The last phase of the labour process, the one which is subject to decay at the moment, is that of the segmentation of labour into three segments (independent primary, subordinate primary and secondary) reinforced by sex and ethnic differences, and resulting in 'class-fraction politics' and working-class weakness. This analysis largely repeats the earlier work of Edwards (1979). There are serious difficulties in applying the segmentation model to the British context. For example, in a major and detailed survey of a local labour market, Blackburn & Mann (1979) found little evidence of labour market segmentation within the male, manual workforce. On the other hand, they did report finding a virtually complete segregation of male and female workers into non-competing groups such that female workers were confined to a secondary labour market. However, there is no reason to suppose that this gender segmentation was an historically emergent labour strategy, rather than the continuation of age-old practices.

Though there are serious conceptual problems with Gordon *et al.*'s work (the tendency to over-simplify, to over-generalise and to confuse levels of analysis; the unsatisfactoriness of the periodisation of capitalism; the failure to deal with the role of the state; the tendency to identify a singular cause of crisis) nevertheless, the work is valuable as an attempt to bring together economic phases, labour process dynamics and labour market structures and to relate them to the changing composition of the working class. Too many analyses posit an unexamined working class, not recognising that the working class has been, and is being, de-composed and re-made under the impact of changing economic conditions, relocation of capital and transformed employer strategies.

Recession and the labour process

The economic slow-down of the late 1970s turned into a full-scale recession between 1978 and 1983. To the worker it meant the dole queue, to the employer over-capacity and rapid redundancies to contain costs. If we focus on Britain's largest exporters, we find that these 55 corporations shed 250,000 jobs between 1978 and 1981, followed by a further 200,000 job losses between 1981 and 1982. More long term, between 1973 and 1982 British Steel, British Leyland, Courtaulds, GKN, Northern Engineering, Dunlop, Massey-Ferguson, Talbot and International Harvester all cut their labour forces *by more than 50%* (*The Financial Times*, 9 Dec 1982).

Of course, redundancies in one large corporation can be soaked up by expansion in other companies. But, overall, this has not happened. Look at the national figures: in September 1978, 22.4 million people had jobs in Britain, 7.1 million in manufacturing industry, 12.9 million in services and 2.4 million in agriculture, mining, construction, etc. Four years later, total employment had shrunk to 20.4 million, consisting of 5.6 million in manufacture, 12.8 million in services and 2 million in the rest. Clearly the service sector is static, whilst everything else about us contracts.

But what does contraction and job loss mean for labour/capital relations? Job insecurity and unemployment are obviously major issues which arouse bitterness, both personally and collectively. Here is how one German steel worker described his feelings when faced with the manifestations of the economic crisis in Germany:

> In almost every company the director's wish is for an additional number of workers to be sacrificed in order to get the stricken ship afloat again. One really has the impression here that the employees are regarded in many plants as unnecessary ballast. Rather like stowaways, they are generously and charitably taken along when things are going well. But when the economy is becalmed, they can simply be thrown overboard to lighten the ship.

(*The Financial Times*, 29 Nov 1978)

Notwithstanding such bitterness, it is typically very difficult for trade unions or other groups to mobilise in order to resist redundancy. Proposed redundancies hit people unevenly, with the result that redundancy is a divisive issue and it becomes difficult to achieve unity. Moreover, in a recession, the power of economic non-cooperation is considerably diluted. If a company wants to reduce the size of its labour-force, then a strike can be self-defeating, particularly if the company can shift production to another plant or another country. In the USA this phenomenon is known as the 'runaway plant'.

Despite media images, trade unions frequently experience a sense of vulnerability. As one author puts it:

> Apart from the rivalry between unions, a vast army of employed are not in unions, there is persistent rank and file resistance to union policies, a variable willingness by workers to act on union decisions and a marked reluctance on the part of some unionists to pay their union dues at all... trade unions are wary of any proposal which could reduce what they see as their precarious hold on events.

(Eccles, 1979, p. 158.)

This felt vulnerability is increased during a recession and pushes trade union representatives towards caution and compromise, towards negotiation with the powers that be. Moreover, trade union officials are often *pulled* in the same direction — by government pressure, by employer threats of total factory closures, by ideological appeals, by the morning newspaper and the night-time brick through the window. Clearly then, redundancies and threats of job-loss do not unite all grades of worker but, on the contrary, leave labour weakened and disorganised. What implications does this carry for employer strategies?

In Chapter 5 we argued that mass unemployment and the weakness of labour indicated above have shifted economic power to the employers so that wage cuts and labour intensifications have become feasible employer strategies. Certainly economic crisis has brought forth management 'hawks'. Here is one company director:

> ...one of the tasks right now is to persuade senior managers to get up and run. There is no lack of know-how. It's a matter of seeing what opportunities there are. We have had a pounding and we are all fed up with it. I think it would be fair to say that it's almost vengeance. ... But take your revenge carefully: most of us have procedure agreements and they have established the mechanisms for challenging management decisions.

(*The Financial Times*, 5 Jan 1981)

But even in these words of a well-known advocate of tighter managerial control, it is possible to discern the dilemma, the contradiction, underlined by this book. Labour cheapening, economic coercion, the direct control methods of Taylorism and Fordism are rarely enough, because all strategies face the contradictory requirements of intensifying control, regulating and dominating the production process, *and* harnessing the ingenuity and cooperativeness of workers. The most fundamental problem of management is the need *simultaneously* to actuate and control the labour force. During economic recessions this dilemma emerges visibly – there is a paradoxical mixture of management aggressiveness and experiments in labour/management cooperation. The contradiction is particularly marked during the 1980s recession because the ground of industrial competition has shifted. As we pointed out in Chapter 5, the Japanese emphasis on a more creative integration of the workforce into the production process has led to significant productivity gains which cannot be ignored by Western manufacturers. Ford of Europe, along with many other industrial corporations, still needs to elicit '100% effort' and worker initiative if it is to eliminate layers of managerial bureaucracy and achieve both flexibility and high quality – all of which is required to face up to Japanese competition and the new market conditions. Ford's 'After Japan' programme is a convenient symbol of the continued pressures for change (see Abernathy, Clark and Kantrow, 1983).

The pressures for change are affecting forms of employment and the labour market as well as the system of management control. Large corporations are seeking to employ the smallest possible core of permanent workers and coping with the inevitable fluctuations in demand by overtime, temporary employment or sub-contracting. Equally, as much indirect work as possible is being hived off to outside contractors, often small companies who specialise in providing maintenance, catering or transport services. Some of these companies in turn utilise 'self-employed' workers, who work long hours under poor conditions (Health and Safety Executive, 1983). The overall impact is to segment the labour force into a series of different labour statuses, a pattern familiar in Japan, with its hierarchy of committed employees with job security, temporary workers, and outside contract workers.

Perhaps the blows of the 1980s recession will re-structure the working class, and create the segmented workforce which Gordon *et al.* (1982) have written about, but which has not been a labour market reality in Britain up to the present.

But there is one more labour status – unemployment. For many millions unemployment is a daily struggle with financial pressures, depression and a sense of worthlessness. The dynamics of the international division of labour during the recession mean that manufacturing corporations are increasingly transferring labour intensive and large-scale production to low wage zones in the Third World, leaving stagnant pools of unemployment in the old industrial economies. Britain, with its heritage of labour intensive manufacturing industry, has yet to resolve how its citizens will spend their working life in the future, and how they will receive the money they need to lead a decent life. For some, the future looks secure. For many others, the future looks bleak – class at work.

References

ABERNATHY, W., CLARK, K., and KANTROW, A., (1983), *Industrial Renaissance*, New York, Basic Books.

ACARD, (1980), *Computer-aided Design and Manufacture*, HMSO.

BABBAGE, C., (1835), 'On the Economy of Machinery and Manufactures', excerpted in DAVIS, L. E. and TAYLOR, J. G. (eds.), (1972), pp. 23-6.

BARRON, I. and CURNOW, R., (1979), *The Future with Microelectronics*, Milton Keynes, The Open University Press.

BARRON, R., and NORRIS, G. M., (1976), 'Sexual Divisions and the Dual Labour Market', in BARKER, D., and ALLEN S.(eds.), *Dependence and Exploitation in Work and Marriage*, Longman, pp. 47-69.

BENDIX, REINHARD, (1974 edition), *Work and Authority in Industry*, University of California Press.

BEYNON, HUW, (1973), *Working for Ford*, Penguin.

BLACKBURN, R. M., and MANN, MICHAEL, (1979), *The Working Class in the Labour Market*, Cambridge University Press.

BLAU, P., (1963), *The Dynamics of Bureaucracy*, University of Chicago Press.

BLAUNER, R., (1960), 'Work Satisfaction and Industrial Trends in Modern Society', in GALENSON, W., and LIPSET, S. M. (eds.), *Labor and Trade Unionism*, Wiley, New York, pp. 473-87.

BRAVERMAN, H., (1974), *Labour and Monopoly Capital*, Monthly Review Press, New York.

BURAWOY, MICHAEL, (1978), 'Towards a Marxist Theory of the Labor Process', *Politics and Society*, 8, pp. 247-312.

BURAWOY, M., (1979), *Manufacturing Consent*, Chicago, University of Chicago Press.

CAVENDISH, R., (1982), *Women on the Line*, Routledge.

CHANDLER, A. D., (1977), *The Visible Hand: The Managerial Revolution in American Business,* Harvard University Press.

CHAPMAN, S. D., (1974), 'The Textile Factory Before Arkwright: A Typology of Factory Development', *Bus.Hist.Review*, 48, pp. 451-78.

CHILD, JOHN, (1969), *British Management Thought*, Allen and Unwin.

COLE, R. E., (1979), *Work, Mobility and Participation: A Comparative Study of American and Japanese Industry,* University of California Press.

COPLEY, F. B., (1915), 'Frederick W. Taylor: Revolutionist', in *The Outlook*, 111, September.

CORRIGAN, PHILIP, (1977), 'Feudal Relics or Capitalist Monuments?', *Sociology*, Vol. 11, No. 3, pp. 411-80.

CRAWCOUR, S., (1978), 'The Japanese Employment System', *Journal of Japanese Studies*, Vol. 4, No. 2, pp. 225-45.

CRESSEY, P., and McINNES, J., (1980), 'Voting for Ford: Industrial Democracy and the Control of Labour', *Capital and Class*, 11, pp. 5-33.

CROZIER, M., (1964), *The Bureaucratic Phenomenon*, Tavistock.

C.S.S., (1981), *New Technology: Society, Employment and Skill*, (C.S.S. Report), Council for Science and Society.

CUTLER, TONY, (1978), 'The Romance of Labour', *Economy and Society*, Vol. 7, No. 1, pp. 74-9.

DAVIS, L. E., (1957), 'Toward a Theory of Job Design', reprinted in DAVIS and TAYLOR, (1972), pp. 215-17.

DAVIS, L. E., (1966), 'The Design of Jobs' reprinted in DAVIS and TAYLOR, (1972), pp. 299-327.

DAVIS, L. E., and TAYLOR, J. C., (1972), *Design of Jobs*, Penguin.

DAVIS, M., (1980), 'Why the U.S. Working Class is Different', *New Left Review*, 123, Sept./Oct., pp. 3-44.

DEACON, ALAN, (1981), 'Unemployment and Politics in Britain since 1945', in SHOWLER, BRIAN, and SINFIELD, ADRIAN (eds.), *The Workless State*, Oxford, Martin Robertson, pp. 59-88.

DEX, S., (1983), 'Recurrent unemployment in young black and white males', *Industrial Relations Journal*, Vol. 14, No. 1, pp. 41-9.

DORE, R. P., (1973), *British Factory – Japanese Factory*, Allen and Unwin.

DOUGLAS, M., (1980), 'Auto workers can only do as well as Head Office permits', *Albuquerque Journal*, 24 July, 1980, p. A5.

DOWNING, H., (1980), 'Word processors and the oppression of women', in FORESTER, T. (1980), pp. 275-89.

DOWNING, H., HOBSON, D., WILLIS, P., and WINSHIP J., (1978), 'Braverman, patriarchal relations, and the deskilling of women's clerical work'. Paper presented at Nuffield Deskilling Conference, mimeo.

DUBIN. R., (1958), *The World of Work*, New Jersey, Prentice-Hall.

ECCLES, T., (1979), 'Control in the Democratized Enterprise: the Case of KME', in PURCELL, J. and SMITH, R. (eds.), *The Control of Work*, Macmillan, pp. 156-77.

EDWARDS, RICHARD, (1979), *Contested Terrain: The Transformation of the Workplace in the Twentieth Century*, Heinemann.

EHRENREICH, J. and EHRENREICH, B., (1976), 'Work and Consciousness', *Monthly Review*, July/Aug., pp. 10-18.

ELGER, A. J., (1975), 'Industrial organisations: a processual perspective,' in MCKINLAY, J. B., (ed.), *Processing People: Cases in Organisational*

Behaviour, Holt, Rinehart and Winston.

ELGER, TONY, (1982), 'Braverman, capital accumulation and deskilling', in WOOD, STEPHEN (ed.), *The Degradation of Work?* Hutchinson, pp. 23-53.

ENGELS, FREDERICK, (1968), 'Socialism, Utopian and Scientific', in MARX and ENGELS, *Selected Works,* Lawrence and Wishart, pp. 375-93.

ELLUL, J., (1964), *The Technological Society,* Vintage Books.

FLECK, J., (1983), 'Robotics in Manufacturing Organisations', in WINCH, G. (1983).

FLINK, J. J., (1975), *The Car Culture,* Boston, MIT Press.

FORD, H., (1922), *My Life and Work,* New York, Doubleday Page.

FORESTER, T., (1980), *The Microelectronics Revolution,* Oxford, Basil Blackwell.

FOX, ALAN, (1974), *Beyond Contract: Work, Power and Trust Relations,* Faber and Faber.

FRANK, ANDRE GUNDER, (1980), *Crisis: in the World Economy,* Heinemann.

FRIDENSON, P., (1978), 'The Coming of the Assembly Line to Europe', in KROHN, LAYTON and WEINGART (eds.), 'The Dynamics of Science and Technology', Utrecht, D. Reidel, pp. 159-75.

FRIEDMAN, A., (1977), 'Responsible Autonomy versus Direct Control', *Capital and Class,* Vol. 1, pp. 43-57.

FROBEL, FOLKER, HEINRICHS, JUGEN, and KREYE, OTTO, (1980), *The New International Division of Labour,* Cambridge University Press.

GINTIS, H., (1976), 'The Nature of Labor Exchange and the Theory of Capitalist Production', *Review of Radical Political Economics,* Summer, Vol. 8, No. 2, pp. 36-54.

GLYN, ANDREW and HARRISON, JOHN, (1980), *The British Economic Disaster,* Pluto Press.

GLYN, ANDREW and SUTCLIFFE, BOB, (1972), *British Capitalism, Workers and the Profit Squeeze,* Penguin.

GOLDING, H., (1933), *The Wonderful World of Machinery,* Ward Lock.

GOLDTHORPE, JOHN, LOCKWOOD, DAVID, BECHHOFER, FRANK, and PLATT, JENNIFER, (1969), *The Affluent Worker in the Class Structure,* Cambridge University Press.

GORDON, D. M., EDWARDS, R., and REICH, M., (1982), *Segmented Work, Divided Workers: the Historical Transformation of Labor in the United States,* Cambridge University Press.

GOSPEL, H. and LITTLER, C. R., (1983), *Managerial Strategies and Industrial Relations,* Heinemann.

GOULDNER, A. W., (1954), *Patterns of Industrial Bureaucracy,* New York, Free Press.

GREEN, K., (1978), 'Group Technology in Small Batch Engineering'. Paper presented at Nuffield Deskilling Conference, mimeo.

HACKMAN, J. R., and OLDHAM, G. R., (1975), 'Development of the Job Diagnostic Survey', *Journal of Applied Psychology*, 60, 2, pp. 159-70.

HANNAH, L., (1976), *The Rise of the Corporate Economy*, Methuen.

HAY-MSL, (1979), *Employee Benefits Survey*, privately published.

HEILBRONER, R. L., (1977), *Business Civilisation in Decline*, Penguin.

HERZBERG, F., (1966), *Work and the Nature of Man*, Cleveland, World Publishing Co.

HERZBERG, F., (1976), *The Managerial Choice: To Be Efficient and To Be Human*, Homewood, Illinois, Dow Jones-Irwin.

HULL, D., (1978), *The Shop Steward's Guide to Work Organization*, Spokesman.

JACKSON, DUDLEY, (1976), 'Pay — How Equal?', *New Society*, March 11.

JENKINS, D., (1978), 'The West German Humanization of Work Programme: A Preliminary Assessment', WRU Occasional Paper No. 8.

KAMATA, SATOSHI, (1982), *Japan in the Passing Lane*, Pantheon.

KATZ, F. E., (1973), 'Integrative and adaptive uses of autonomy: worker autonomy in factories,' in SALAMAN, G. and THOMPSON, K. (eds.), *People and Organisations*, Longman, pp. 190-204.

KELLY, J. E., (1982), *Scientific Management, Job Redesign and Work Performance*, Academic Press.

LEFFINGWELL, W. H., (1917), *Scientific Office Management*, A. W. Shaw.

LEFFINGWELL, W. H., (1925), *Office Management: Principles and Practice*, A. W. Shaw.

LEVINE, S. B. and KAWADA, H., (1980), 'Human Resources in Japanese Industrial Development', Princeton University Press.

LEWCHUK, W., (1983), 'Fordism and British Motor Car Employers, 1896-1932', in GOSPEL, H. & LITTLER, C. K. (eds), (1983), pp. 82-110.

LIBERAL INDUSTRIAL INQUIRY, (1928), *Britain's Industrial Future*, Liberal Party.

LINHART, R., (1981), *The Assembly Line*, John Calder.

LIPIETZ, A., (1982), 'Towards Global Fordism?', *New Left Review*, 132, Mar/April, pp. 33-47.

LITTLER, C. R., (1978), 'Understanding Taylorism', *British Journal of Sociology*, 29, pp. 185-202.

LITTLER, C. R., (1982), *The Development of the Labour Process in Capitalist Societies*, Heinemann.

LITTLER, C. R., (1983), 'A comparative analysis of managerial structures and strategies', in GOSPEL, H. and LITTLER, C. R. (eds.), (1983), pp. 171-96.

LITTLER, C. R. and SALAMAN, G., (1982), 'Bravermania and Beyond: Recent Theories of the Labour Process', *Sociology*, 16, 2, May, pp. 251-69.

LOCKETT, M. and LITTLER, C. R., (1984), *Management and Industry in China*, Heinemann.

LOCKWOOD, D., (1958), *The Blackcoated Worker,* Allen and Unwin.

MANDEL, ERNEST, (1978), *Late Capitalism,* New Left Review Editions, Verso Books, London.

MARQUAND, JUDITH, (1967), 'Which are the lower paid workers?', *British Journal of Industrial Relations,* V, 3, Nov., pp. 359-74.

MARSH, P., (1981), *The Silicon Chip Book,* Sphere Books.

MARX, KARL, (1968), 'Wages, Price and Profit', in MARX and ENGELS, *Selected Works,* Lawrence and Wishart, pp. 185-226.

McCRACKEN, PAUL, (1977), *Towards Full Employment and Price Stability,* Paris, OECD.

METCALF, DAVID, (1980), 'Unemployment. History, incidence and prospects', *Policy and Politics,* 8:1, pp. 21-37.

MEYER, S., (1981), *The Five-Dollar Day: Labor Management and Social Control in the Ford Motor Co., 1908-21,* State University of New York Press.

MILLS, C. WRIGHT, (1951), *White Collar,* Oxford, Oxford University Press.

NEW SOCIETY, (1979), 'The Unequal Ranks of Workers', *New Society,* August 9.

NICHOLS, THEO, (1980), *Capital and Labour: A Marxist Primer,* Fontana.

NICHOLS, T., (1978), *Current Controversies in Class and Stratification Theory,* Open University Course D 207, Unit 13, Milton Keynes, The Open University Press.

NICHOLS, THEO, and ARMSTRONG, PETER, (1973), *Safety or Profit,* Bristol, Falling Wall Press.

NICHOLS, T. and BEYNON, H., (1977), *Living With Capitalism,* Routledge.

NOLAN, P. and EDWARDS, P. K., (1982), 'Homogenize, Divide and Rule: an essay on segmented work, divided workers'. Mimeo.

NORRIS, G. M., (1978), 'Industrial Paternalist Capitalism and Local Labour Markets', *Sociology,* 12, 3, pp. 469-90.

OFFE, C., (1976), *Industry and Inequality,* Edward Arnold.

OFFICE OF MANPOWER ECONOMICS, (1973), *Measured Daywork,* HMSO.

OSORIO, U. J., (1975), 'Superexplotacion y clase obrera: el caso mexicano', *Cuadernos Politicos,* Mexico, no. 6, Octubre.

O'TOOLE, JAMES, (1981), *Making America Work: Productivity and Responsibility,* New York, Continuum.

PALM, GORAN, (1977), *The Flight from Work,* Cambridge University Press.

PALMER, BRYAN, (1975), 'Class, Conception and Conflict: The Thrust for Efficiency. Managerial Views of Labour and Working Class Rebellion 1903-22', *The Review of Radical Political Economics,* 7, pp. 31-49.

PERROW, CHARLES, (1972), *Complex Organisations: A Critical Essay,* Glenview, Illinois, Scott, Foresman.

PETERSON, S., (1965), 'Corporate Control and Capitalism', *Quarterly Journal of Economics*, 79/1.

POULANTZAS, N., (1975), *Classes in Contemporary Capitalism*, New Left Books.

PRAIS, S. J., (1976), *The Evolution of Giant Firms in Britain*, Cambridge University Press.

PRANDY, KENNETH, (1979), 'Ethnic Discrimination in Employment and Housing', *Ethnic and Racial Studies*, Vol. 2, No. 1, pp. 66-79.

ROETHLISBERGER, F. J., and DICKSON, W., (1964), *Management and the Worker*, Wiley.

ROSE, M., (1975), *Industrial Behaviour: Theoretical Developments since Taylor*, Allen Lane.

ROUTH, G., (1966), *Occupation and Pay in Britain 1906-60*, Cambridge University Press.

ROY, D., (1973), 'Banana time: job satisfaction and informal interaction', in SALAMAN, G. and THOMPSON, K. (eds.), *People and Organisations*, Longman, pp. 205-22.

ROYAL COMMISSION ON THE DISTRIBUTION OF INCOME AND WEALTH, (1978), background paper, No. 5, HMSO.

RUSSELL, BERTRAND, (1932), *In Praise of Idleness*, Allen & Unwin.

RUSSELL, J., (1978), 'The Coming of the Line: The Ford Highland Park Plant, 1910-14', in *Radical America*, 12, pp. 29-45.

SABEL, C. F., (1982), *Work and Politics*, Cambridge University Press.

SALAMAN, GRAEME, (1979), *Work Organisations, Resistance and Control*, Longman.

SAVALL, H., (1981), *Work and People*, Clarendon Press.

SCOTT, JOHN, (1979), *Corporations, Classes and Capitalism*, Hutchinson.

SINFIELD, ADRIAN, (1981), *What Unemployment Means*, Oxford, Martin Robertson.

SMITH, ADAM, (1776, 1970 edn.), *The Wealth of Nations*, Penguin.

SOFFER, B., (1960), 'A Theory of Trade Union Development: The Role of the "Autonomous" Workman', *Labor History*, 1, pp. 141-63.

STARK, D., (1978), *Class Structure, Class Struggle and the Labor Process*, Harvard University, nimeo.

STINCHCOMBE, A. L., (1974), *Creating Efficient Industrial Administrations*, New York, Academic Press.

TAKAGI, I., (1982), 'Corporate labor policies in flux', in *Economic Eye*, 3, 4, December, pp. 16-19.

TAYLOR, F. W., (1903), *Shop Management*, reprinted in TAYLOR, 1964.

TAYLOR, F. W., (1911), *The Principles of Scientific Management*, reprinted in TAYLOR, 1964.

TAYLOR, F. W., (1964), *Scientific Management,* Harper & Row.

TAYLOR, J. C., (1979), 'Job design criteria twenty years later', in DAVIS, L. E. and TAYLOR, J. C. (eds.), *Design of Jobs,* 2nd edn., Santa Monica, Goodyear.

TAYLOR, ROBERT, (1982), *Workers and the New Depression,* Macmillan.

THOMPSON, E. P., (1967), 'Time, Work-Discipline and Industrial Capitalism' in *Past & Present: A Journal of Historical Studies,* 38, pp. 56-97.

THOMPSON, PAUL, (1983), *The Nature of Work,* Macmillan.

THUROW, LESTER C., (1981), 'Death by a Thousand Cuts', *New York Review of Books,* Vol. XXVIII, No. 20.

TOURAINE, ALAIN, (1971), *The Post-Industrial Society,* Random House, New York.

TURNER, B., (1970), 'The Organization of Production: scheduling in Complex Batch Production situations' in HEALD, G. (ed.), *Approaches to the Study of Organizational Behaviour,* Tavistock, pp. 87-99.

WALLERSTEIN, IMMANUEL, (1974), *The Modern World System,* New York, Academic Press.

WALTON, R. E., (1974), 'Innovative Restructuring of Work' in ROSOW, J. (ed.), *The Worker and the Job: Coping with Change,* New Jersey, Prentice Hall.

WEDDERBURN, DOROTHY, and CRAIG, ROSEMARY, (1974), 'Relative Deprivation in Work', in Wedderburn, D. (ed.), *Poverty, Inequality and Class Structure,* Cambridge University Press, pp. 141-64.

WESTERGAARD, JOHN, and RESLER, HENRIETTA, (1975), *Class in a Capitalist Society,* Heinemann.

WHITE, M. and TREVOR, M., (1983), *Under Japanese Management,* Heinemann.

WILKINSON, B., (1983), *The Shop-floor Politics of New Technology,* Heinemann.

WILSON, N. A. B., (1973), 'On the Quality of Working Life', Manpower Papers No. 7, HMSO.

WINCH, G., (1982), 'Bargaining over technological change,' mimeo.

WINCH, G., (1983), *Information Technology in the Manufacturing Industries,* Rossendale.

WOOD, S., (1982), *The Degradation of Work?* Hutchinson.

WORK IN AMERICA, (1973), Report of a Special Task Force to the Secretary of Health, Education & Welfare, Boston, MIT Press.

WRIGHT, E. O., (1975), 'Alternative Perspectives in Marxist Theories of Accumulation Crisis,' *Insurgent Sociologist,* Vol. 6, 1, pp. 5-39.

WRIGHT, E. O., (1976), 'Class Boundaries in Advanced Capitalist Societies', *New Left Review,* July/Aug. 1976, pp. 3-41.

WRIGHT, E. O., (1980), 'Class, Occupation & Organization' in DUNKERLY, D. and SALAMAN, G. *The International Yearbook of Organization Studies,* Routledge, pp. 1-30.

ZERMENO. R., MOSELEY, R. and BRAUN, E., (1980), 'The robots are coming – slowly' in FORESTER, T. (1980), pp. 184-97.
ZIMBALIST, A. (ed.), (1979), *Case Studies On the Labor Process,* Monthly Review Press.

Index